Patches of Joy

Patches of Joy

Velma Seawell Daniels

Foreword by
FRANK G. SLAUGHTER

PELICAN PUBLISHING COMPANY
GRETNA 1976

Library of Congress Cataloging in Publication Data

Daniels, Velma Seawell.
    Patches of joy.
        1. Daniels, Velma Seawell.   2. Christian life—
Baptist authors.   I. Title.
BX6495.D3A35   286'.1'0924 [B]   76-4773
ISBN 0-88289-101-4

First Printing: September, 1976
Second Printing: Prior to publication, September, 1976

Manufactured in the United States of America

Designed by Oscar Richard

Published by Pelican Publishing Company, Inc.
630 Burmaster Street, Gretna, Louisiana 70053

To many friends—one in particular.
How difficult to select a few friends
to tell about.
The selection of some is not intended
to be the rejection of any.

Contents

Foreword

Patches of Joy is almost as charming and delightful as its author, with this difference: the book is "patches," a lot of them and all telling a joyful story, but Velma Daniels is joy all the time. She radiates it, in person, in writing, from the television screen, in everything she does.

To her, sharing what she believes in and trusts implicitly, her faith in God and those created in his image, is more important than anything else in life. So it was natural that her faith and the joy it gives her should bubble over into this delightful book about people she knows, experiences she's had, and most of all the joy of sharing.

Books like *Patches of Joy* don't come along very often because people capable of writing them are pretty scarce. Fortunately there's one of them at least who's generous enough to share the sources of her own joy and faith.

FRANK G. SLAUGHTER

Welcome

Thanks for picking up my book!

It was written especially for YOU.

As you read it, I hope it will make you feel good. I felt good when I wrote it, for it is all about the joys of life. When people have joy in their lives, you can tell it in their walk, you can tell it in their talk, and you can tell it in the sunshine of their smiles.

Joy! It is something that we can all have. We don't have to wait until the tomorrows. We don't have to wait until our jobs are better, or our children are grown, or when we can afford to do this or that.

No, joy is today! It is ours just for the asking.

In this book about the joys in life, I talk about some of the people I have known. Some of them are old friends. Some are casual acquaintances. Some of them are well known, but most of them are people you have never heard of before. Each of them, in a positive way, has influenced my thinking.

I bring you the stories of people who have discovered this "joy" that we are talking about. I bring you these stories with the prayer that the candles they have lit with their lives might help brighten your pathway.

That's what *Patches of Joy* is all about.

11

Patches of Joy

Joy on the Grapevine

"Hello, Johnnie May. It's me, Jewel. . . . Oh, just fine, thanks. Did Aubrey get off on the plane all right? . . . That's fine. It will be nice to have her with you while he's away. . . . Me? Not exactly good. . . . Sick? Oh, no. It's this new apartment. . . . I know right now that I'm not going to like it. Imagine, the third floor, and my only view is the backside of another building. . . . Yes, that's true, I didn't like the sixth floor, but that was because of the morning sun. Remember? . . . That ground floor we had? No, thanks. That one backed up on the shopping center parking lot. . . . Maybe you're right, Johnnie May, but I'll tell you one thing. This is the worst I've seen."

You can be assured that Johnnie May's day has been pretty well battered, if not ruined. She will be sharing her friend's discontent for the next several hours.

Whenever you put bad news on the grapevine, you infect everyone along the line with your unhappiness.

Joy works the same way. Put a little of it on the

15

grapevine, and you can spread good cheer and happiness all over the place.

I have a friend who does that. You may have heard of him, Dr. Hans Hannau. He is recognized as one of the world's most innovative photographers. His beautiful *USA in Full Color* is only one of more than sixty-five picture travel books he has published.

As he travels the world, he conveys excitement and contentment. His readers feel this verve and love of life and satisfaction through the dramatics of his camera.

Once when I interviewed him on a television program, he summed up his philosophy. "My mother taught me," he said, "always to heed the words of the Apostle Paul, '. . . for I have learned, in whatsoever state I am, therewith to be content.'"

A casual observer might say, "That's easy for him. He's famous and rich." But that is here and now. To arrive, Dr. Hannau had to travel a road that would have defeated most stout men.

Look back to Vienna just prior to World War II. Young Hannau had just received his doctorate in law and was working for the government. He worked diligently against the Nazis, and when Hitler marched into Austria, Dr. Hannau was arrested and confined in the dread concentration camp—Buchenwald. Due to a peculiar circumstance, which he says was "the hand of God at work," Dr. Hannau was released for three days—time enough for him to flee to the United States with his family.

Once here, penniless, he relied on his youthful hobby of photography as a livelihood. His work took him to Miami Beach, where he studied hard to learn English. Try as he might, he was not able to erase his heavy German accent. When the United States entered

the war, he was jailed as a spy. "After all," the government authorities reasoned, "he was seen taking pictures
all day long and he spoke with a thick accent."

"But," he said, "I never complained. My greatest
humiliation came when my wife had to work as a maid
to support our two children while I was not able to earn
a living."

Dr. Hannau was eventually cleared of the false
charges and managed to eke out the war years taking
pictures.

In the early 1950s, when the hotel boom hit Miami
Beach, he saw the need for high-quality photography to
help promote the tourist trade. With that in mind, he
talked to the owner of one of the newest and finest
hotels on the beach. The man gave him an oral go-ahead
to produce a colored brochure. This was to be his "big
break" he thought, so he invested all of his savings in
special camera equipment and went to work. He spent
several weeks making the color transparencies, using a
technique he had invented for lighting and photo-
graphing large interiors. Finally, when the photographs
were ready and his colorful layouts had been properly
mounted, he took them to the hotel owner.

"What beautiful work," the hotel man told him.
"But the cost is prohibitive. Forget it."

"Forget it? I can't forget it. I have hundreds of
dollars invested in this work. You told me to go ahead
with it. You gave me an oral contract."

"I changed my mind," the man said. "Good-bye.
And don't waste your time suing me. You won't get a
dime."

"I was sick," Dr. Hannau recalled. "I sat in my car
and nearly cried. How could I tell my wife? All our
savings gone—for nothing. Then I thought of other times

when life had looked bleak. This situation called for an extra effort from me.

"I'll always remember that day. I left his office about two o'clock. As I sat in my car, discouraged and defeated, I reminded myself that I was a Christian. My Christian teaching had shown me that bitterness would do me no good. So I asked God to help me. I put myself in his hands and asked him to help me make the proper move. I thought of my mother saying when I was a boy, 'The Lord helps those who help themselves.' I decided to get busy.

"I still had several working hours before I had to face my family in defeat, so I called at another of the new hotels on my way home. I showed the owner my beautiful layouts."

The rest of his story sounds like a page from one of Horatio Alger's books. That hotel man declared, "If this is the sort of brochure that the hotel people are having printed, I'll have to get one even better. How soon can you start work on mine?"

Flushed with success, Dr. Hannau visited three other hotel owners before the close of business that day, and walked away with an order from each of them. Suddenly he was in business—publishing colored brochures. He was on the way to a highly successful career as a photographer, writer, and publisher of some of the most beautiful travel books in the world.

Think what would have happened if Dr. Hannau had allowed the discouragement of that first hotel man to destroy his faith? What would have happened if he had let that word of rejection and refusal permeate his spirit?

Now, as I write these lines, two of Dr. Hannau's lovely books rest on my coffee table. To me they symbolize the grapevine of his life, bringing beauty and color wherever they go, and carrying with them a message of great Christian fortitude, hope, and joy.

"Ain't No Spitbacks, Lady!"

Mrs. Roberta Hancock had moved into our neighborhood that afternoon and was busy sorting through packing crates when the doorbell rang. There stood a little five-year-old neighbor boy holding a tray of party sandwiches. "Miz Hancock," he announced, "my mom had a coffee hour this morning and she thought you might like some of these sandwiches." He handed them to Roberta and turned to leave. As he started down the steps, he called over his shoulder, "Miz Hancock, those are leftovers, but there ain't no spit-backs!"

Roberta was still laughing at the youngster's remark three days later when she sat in my kitchen getting acquainted over a cup of tea. "Spitback," she said. "I never heard that expression before. What does it mean?"

I had to tell her that I didn't know and it was just a slang expression. Then I recalled the only time I had ever heard the word. The remembrance of that occasion brought a lump to my throat and a tear to my eye.

I was attending college at the time and had been invited to teach a Sunday-school class of nine-year-old girls. That was my first teaching experience, and those girls became like little sisters to me. One day after we had finished with our Bible lesson, we were talking about talents. We were discussing how God had given each one of us a different talent. I told them that God wants each of us to do something special for him. I explained that every single job is as important as any other.

One little girl spoke up and said, "I want to be a preacher!" Another said, "I want to be a mommy and bring my children to Sunday school." As we went around the room from girl to girl, one who was rather shabbily dressed hung her head and said, "I guess God forgot to give me any talents, 'cause I'm just a spit-back."

Almost instantly, Mary Susan, who was sitting next to her, said, "I just want to LIVE for Jesus, and any-body can do that! You can do that. Anybody can do that." She took her little friend's hand, and I shall never forget the look on that child's face as it brightened, as she realized that, yes, indeed, "anybody can do that!"

Later that year, Mary Susan accepted the Lord as her personal Savior. She led the way to the altar early one Sunday morning as one by one the others followed to make their profession of faith.

God worked wonders in that Sunday-school class. Sandy did not grow up to be a preacher, but she did go to Honduras twenty-three years later to help rebuild a church that had been destroyed by a hurricane. One by one, each child grew into a Christian woman and took her own place in her church.

And through the years, Mary Susan's testimony stayed with me. "I just want to LIVE for Jesus."

While in college, Mary Susan married a football star. One weekend when they were enroute to visit a friend, their automobile was struck by a speeding train. They died instantly. Though it happened in another state, I was notified immediately. The moment I heard the tragic news, her testimony flashed before me: "I just want to LIVE for Jesus."

She had lived for Jesus! Now she had been called to greater glory. I knew Jesus had swept her up in his arms the instant the train struck her car, saying, "You were only nine years old, my child, and indeed you kept your promise. You have LIVED for me. This is your reward!"

At the funeral service for Mary Susan, I saw the young woman who had called herself a "spitback." "I remember that day well," she said. "That was the day Mary Susan explained the true message of Jesus Christ and gave my life a sense of purpose."

How true the scripture is that tells us, ". . . And a child shall lead them."

Those Blessed Bonfires

The postman handed me a small envelope embossed in gold script letters: "Mrs. George Wallace, Executive Mansion, Montgomery, Alabama." I tore the envelope open. It was a warm, breezy invitation to my husband and me to visit her.

"What a thoughtful note," I said to myself as I reread it. Mrs. Cornelia Wallace, the First Lady of Alabama, was a long-time friend of mine. We first became acquainted when she moved to Florida to become a skier and model at Cypress Gardens. Through these many years, I recognized Cornelia as the treasured kind of friend that never changes. Her religion gives her strength for her day. Her spiritual priorities take first place in her life.

I never get over being shocked when I hear people say, "What faith Mrs. Wallace must have! You wonder why she hasn't gone to pieces during the governor's long convalescence." But I am not amazed at her endurance. God, to whom Cornelia continually gives credit for her faith, began long ago to prepare her for this part of her life. A critic once said of Rubens: "He was a great painter, but he lacked that last undefinable something which makes heart speak to heart. You admire, but you never adore. No real sorrow ever entered his life." Cornelia Wallace has experienced more than her share of loss and sorrow.

Early in life she decided on a career in music. But while in New York pursuing her ambition, her father, Charles G. Ellis, became gravely ill with cancer, and she returned to her home in Montgomery. Cornelia remained at his bedside until he died. She was then only twenty-one years old. His lingering death left deep and painful scars. Her family suggested that a job in Florida might serve as a healing tonic. And so she came. Months later she married John Snively III. They had two sons, but the marriage ended in divorce. Heartbroken, Cornelia left Florida and returned with her children to her mother's home in Montgomery. More sorrows came to her when her beloved stepfather, Dr. Burton Austin, also died of cancer.

On January 4, 1971, Cornelia married Governor Wallace. Sixteen months later, on May 15, 1972, an assassin's bullet felled him during a political speech in Maryland. Months, perhaps years, of suffering and pain lay ahead for the governor; and for Cornelia, the anguish of watching her husband struggle to retain his position of leadership.

The night of the shooting, prayer chains for the governor's recovery were started throughout the country, at the request of Cornelia Wallace. She maintains that without prayer she could not have survived those first dark hours.

God had prepared the First Lady of Alabama to face another time of trial. Through his power, she transmitted strength and assurance to the other members of the family.

Clare Boothe Luce, while consoling a friend once, said, "A great grief is a tremendous bonfire in which all the trash of life is consumed." Cornelia Wallace has endured many bonfires. Each has fortified and reenforced her faith.

I thought of Cornelia's faith that morning when her note arrived, and found joy and peace as I remembered the Twenty-third Psalm as it reads in *The Living Bible*: "Because the Lord is my Shepherd, I have everything I need." Yes, even when those bonfires burn.

Some Mule in Every Boy

"Daddy, I can't take a dime to Sunday school anymore," the little fellow said. "I need a quarter from now on, because the teacher said that the Juniors are going UP today." He got his quarter, even though he had misinterpreted his teacher's announcement concerning Promotion Day.

Once there was another boy—he is a grown man now—who started with a dime. His dime grew into a quarter, and that quarter grew into dollars—millions of dollars.

George Washington Jenkins came to Florida from Warm Springs, Georgia, in 1925 with only nine dollars in his pocket. Today he serves as chairman of the Executive Committee of Publix Super Markets, Inc. He started this great chain of food stores in a small grocery in Winter Haven. His first store wasn't even on a corner.

Even in those days, he had learned that weekly specials brought thrifty housewives to his store. Once when he had advertised freshly ground coffee for 21 cents a pound, the newspaper mistakenly reversed the figures. Typical of George Jenkins, he took a deep breath and said he'd grind coffee that day for 12 cents. When he opened his store Saturday morning, twenty-seven women were waiting for coffee. He often laughs about that day. "Twenty-seven women," he says. "I remember counting them. My store was so small that only fifteen of them could get inside at one time. So most of the day I had a line standing outside. I sure learned about the power of advertising that day."

From that modest beginning, he parlayed his enterprise into a multi-million-dollar business that includes more than two hundred stores. He made his slogan, "where shopping is a pleasure," the byword for thousands of housewives.

As salt and pepper savor food, two ingredients spiced George Jenkins' rise to success—a vision and humility.

His business thrived because, above all else, he sought to please his customers.

He did not begin his career as a supermarket executive. When shoppers in the early days were assisted to their cars with their groceries, the bag boy often was George Jenkins himself. A rule he worked by came from the old slogan "I'll never ask a man to do a job I won't do myself."

In his dreams, he saw a day when women would enjoy doing their marketing instead of looking on it as a wearisome chore. He visualized attractive markets, well lighted and sparkling clean with wide aisles and plenty of service personnel.

Yes, he had the vision and humility, but in those days he lacked capital and the encouragement of financial backers. However, there is some mule in every boy. George Jenkins determined to see his dreams come true. And, by George (and nobody else), he did it.

He will tell you that his success came from hard work. His close friends and his oldest employees give credit to his basic understanding and compassion for the people around him. Early in his business career, he settled on a formula for inspiring and motivating his employees: "I'll let them share in any success I might have." And a profit-sharing plan was born. He figured that if every employee owned a portion of the company, they would be more interested in the welfare of the business—their business. The idea worked. Because George Jenkins cared first for his employees, his business boomed from that one-room store into an enterprise that grosses more than a billion dollars annually.

Profit sharing is not new. The greatest business on earth works on that basis—God's business. Profit sharing with Him reaches such magnitude that it can't be measured. It staggers the mind of man. It stretches beyond man's ability to comprehend.

Because, if you are a good steward, a good worker in God's vineyard, you will receive your share of the profits.

Every employee does not need to understand the total operation of the sprawling grocery empire of George Jenkins in order to share in its profits. And every Christian does not need to understand everything in the Bible in order to share in God's love. We do not need to understand the total meaning of the Revelation. God does not demand that we comprehend the full essence of his Gospel. He only asks that we believe. He only calls on us to accept Jesus Christ as our Savior.

When we do that, we'll receive our profit—Eternal Life.

How is that for profit sharing?

Jesus said, "Ye shall know them by their fruits." In the case of George Jenkins, by his fruits, meats, milk products, and other fine foods.

Quietude on Iron Mountain

"Strange, isn't it? Folks don't come up here as much as they used to."

Though the voice was quiet, it startled me. I had not heard the bent, little old man approaching. The pathways around Bok Tower were matted with brown pine needles that muffled the sound of steps. I had been sitting on a bench waiting for my guests to tour the grounds, and in the solitude my thoughts had drifted elsewhere.

The man who spoke to me was one of the caretakers who keeps the gardens so perfectly manicured.

After returning his greeting, I said, "I noticed there were only a dozen or so people here today, but I thought maybe it was because it's a weekday."

"No," he replied. "All the days are alike now. Folks used to come and take pictures and spend the whole day just looking at the birds, the trees, and the flowers here on Iron Mountain. But it seems like folks don't like quiet places anymore. Most folks go where the crowds are. And you know, lady, the folks who do come aren't happy like they used to be. Don't know what the trouble is, but seems like to me the whole world has lost the joy of the Lord, somewhere along the way."

His voice reflected the sadness in his heart, as he stuck his pointed stick into a piece of paper that some careless visitor had thrown on the ground.

My new friend appeared to be lonely, and I was glad to have him to talk to. He seemed troubled not only about the situation at the sanctuary, but about things in general.

I replied, "I love to come here. When I was a little girl, we spent most Sunday afternoons here, and my parents would explain how Mr. Edward Bok had come to this country from Holland, and had made this wonderful place for others to visit and meditate in and enjoy. Did you know Mr. Bok?"

"Yes, ma'am. He loved this place so much that he wanted to share it with everyone. He was a kind man. I know one thing—he was good to me. I have a job here as long as I live." He needed someone to talk to, and I was glad to listen. "Ma'am," he said, "see those giant iron doors that open into the tower? Did you know there are thirty separate panels that tell the story of the Creation?"

He leaned on a nearby oak tree to rest and continued his narrative about Bok Tower. "Mr. Bok wanted to make this place for quietness so that people whose minds and bodies were tired could come and sit a spell and do some real healin'-thinkin'."

There were other things I wanted to ask him, but just then the carillon bells interrupted with the afternoon concert. He waved good-bye with his soiled old cap and moved away to finish his job of cleaning up.

I started to raise my hand to stop him. After all, I

had not even gotten his name. But I stopped short, because when the chimes peal out over the countryside from the majestic 205-foot tower, there is a reverence that falls over the grounds.

My new friend had enriched my day. I sat there awhile, musing over what he had said. Has the world really become such a beehive that we have forgotten how to be alone? Have we forgotten how to listen to the song of a bird, or the whistle of the wind through the pines? Have we forgotten the joy of finding the remains of a hatched eggshell or discovering a nest of wood ducks in the hollow of a fallen tree? I wondered what the little old caretaker had meant when he said, "The world has lost the joy of the Lord."

The bells were still pealing out their beautiful music as I left my bench and strolled along the path bordering the reflecting pool that caresses the foot of Bok Tower.

Then suddenly the bells stopped ringing. The world was quiet. The only sound between the earth and heaven came from the throat of a nearby tree frog—probably crying "encore, encore."

My thoughts had been racing side by side with the musical notes of the carillon. When the bells stopped, so did my meditations.

All at once I found myself studying the reflection of the tower as it looked at itself in the pool. Then, overcome with awe and reverence, I heard a hushed voice. It was speaking to me. Only to me, for no one else was there.

"Be still and know that I am God."

Sprinkled with Pixie Dust

"Yonder over there are growing the most beautiful lilies anywhere in the world," my native guide explained as I looked over the crest of a hill at sundown in Bermuda. "Perfume made from these lilies is flown all over the world."

My guide had no formal education, but he knew the story of his island better than any book could tell it. He spoke with fervor and eagerness and pride. He made me fall in love with Bermuda.

As I stood listening to him, I recalled listening to another spellbinder when I was a little girl. I was enchanted then by Tinker Bell, the tiny fairy in the great children's classic, *Peter Pan*. I loved her and everything she said—because she spread faith and trust, and a sprinkling of "pixie dust." I couldn't help thinking that my guide, too, had mastered the art of sprinkling "pixie dust."

Pixie dust can turn the ordinary into the extraordinary. With a wee pinch of it we can make a dull common task glow and become an exciting happening.

There are many ways to spread pixie dust. We have our own unique way of touching others with joy and happiness. We might do it with a kind word or a song or a birthday card or flowers.

Like my mother.

I can never remember a time when she did not work on our church flower committee. Those ladies keep busy. Oh, do they love their work. I never saw a happier group of women. Every day they carry bouquets to people in the hospital—and not just to members of their own church, either. Their flowers brighten the homes of shut-ins and the bereaved all over town.

The flowers come from the gardens of church members. The committee has a system of collecting them, trimming and sorting them, and making them into attractive arrangements. They claim they do this to save money, but I think there is more to it than that. The benefits of their little plan go beyond any financial consideration.

I've thought of it many times, and I'm sure pixie dust comes in there somewhere.

Flowers seem to be covered with the stuff. You can't pick up a flower without getting some on you. And when you hand a flower to a friend, some of it gets on him, too.

The way I figure it, the people who package the seeds, the people who plant the gardens and raise the flowers, the ladies who cut and trim and deliver the flowers, the folks who receive them and share them with their friends, all get a sprinkling along the way.

Of course, spreading pixie dust is not a new idea.

David did it. In one of his glorious psalms, he urges us as happy people to worship God with a cheerful spirit as we sing: "Make a joyful noise unto the Lord. . . .

Serve the Lord with gladness; come before his presence with singing."

So whether you do it with words, like my Bermuda guide, or with flowers, like the church committee, or with a song, like David, start sprinkling pixie dust wherever you go.

But I'd better warn you about something. Once you sprinkle it, pixie dust won't rub off. It just sticks, and sticks, and sticks—all day long.

I Am Only One

"Good morning," I said to the lady on the porch as I opened my front door in response to the chimes. "Hello."

Then, sputtering with embarrassment, I said, "Why, look who's here. Pat Anderson. Welcome back. Welcome home. Come in. Come in. Let me put the coffee on."

I'm sure that the hug I gave her was a little too tight and the kiss on her cheek a bit too warm. I hustled her into the living room, sat her down, and fled to the kitchen to put on the coffee and regain my composure.

Two minutes later, when I returned to the living room wearing my best welcome-home smile, I was in control. I only hoped she had not noticed the strange look I must have had when I opened the door. I'm sure it was there, because I had not recognized her—one of my dearest friends, my college roommate, a woman I had waved good-bye to at the airport only three months before.

This clear-eyed, vivacious, cheerful woman, sitting here so straight and with such an air of eagerness, couldn't be the one I had given a bon voyage party for just weeks ago. That woman's face had been lined with despair, and her shoulders had drooped with the weight of the world. I had found it almost impossible to look into her eyes, because the fear and hopelessness I saw there were calling for help I didn't know how to give.

When I took her to the airport the next day, I said good-bye to a friend who had experienced a divorce, the trauma of having to commit a retarded child, sudden financial loss, and a death in her immediate family, all within six months. A woman whose burdens seemed so great that she had fallen into a deep state of melancholia.

Her doctor had urged her to "get away for a while," if she could. Luckily she had received an invitation to visit a friend who was on a job assignment in Iran. Several of her close friends and I had insisted that she go. That's probably putting it mildly, because really we packed her up and sent her.

Now she was back—a completely new woman.

"Oh," I said, "I'm so glad to see you. How wonderful you look. I've never seen such a change in anybody in such a short time. You know, I didn't recognize you when I opened the door."

"I know," she said. "You looked flustered. That was the nicest compliment I've had all day."

"Tell me all about everything," I said. "You look great. Travel certainly does agree with you."

"It wasn't the travel itself that helped me," she said, "as much as it was an experience I had in Rome."

"I didn't know you were in Rome. I thought you went to Iran."

"I did, at first. I went from here to Iran to visit Jan. But in spite of everything, I couldn't snap out of it. I

knew I wasn't being very pleasant company, so after
three weeks I decided to move on. I realized I needed
to be alone. Completely alone to think and to rest and
not have to talk to people or be on a time schedule.
You know I've always wanted to visit the Holy Land, so
I went to Israel. I stayed a month. But I was restless and
wasn't able to rid myself of my depression. So I decided
to fly to Rome. And that's where it all happened."

"Whatever it was," I said, "it certainly did turn you
back into the old Pat I used to know. What was it? What
happened?"

"The whole incident was strange in a way," she explained. "I suppose I was ready for it. I had been resting
and relaxing and thinking for nearly two months, so
my mind must have been more receptive than usual.
Anyway, I had been sightseeing all over Rome and
ended up one afternoon in Saint Peter's Cathedral.
After following the directions in the guidebook for an
hour or more, I suddenly found myself standing in front
of that beautiful sculpture by Michelangelo—the Pieta.

"As I stood there, the most peculiar sensation swept
through me, as though the scene were real. As if Mary,
holding her crucified son, were alive. I could feel her
heartache and her misery and emptiness. Then the tears
came. Her agony became mine. I thought of my own
problems and how they came to nothing with hers.

"I don't know how long I stood there," Pat continued. "Maybe ten minutes. Maybe an hour. I don't
remember. I finally turned toward the doorway in a
sort of trance. As I walked out into the bright light of
the afternoon sun, I came to myself. What had caused
me to stand in front of a marble statue and weep? What
sort of man could transmit such powerful feelings and
emotions through a block of cold stone? Who was this
man Michelangelo?

"As I walked away from Saint Peter's Square, I passed a kiosk where postcards and souvenirs were sold. I stopped to look and found what I wanted—a book about Michelangelo. I sat up most of the night reading about him. I found that his life had been filled with disappointments too. He faced setbacks and opposition and all manner of discouraging problems. I read how many times fate had intervened to divert his attention from his main purpose and how he never wavered and always kept his main goal in sight. I pictured him as he lay in the freezing cold on his back, painting the ceiling of the Sistine Chapel. And I saw him still active and working at the age of eighty-nine with his greatest achievement unfinished—the completion of Saint Peter's.

"That's the experience I had. Two things came out of it. I came to see that my problems are small, really, in the face of my total life. I found that I had been making my own misery. And I learned that I must quit feeling sorry for myself and find something to keep me busy."

"You are absolutely right," I told her. "Sometimes it takes a serious shakeup to find the truth."

"I came to tell you about it first thing," Pat went on. "I want you to know what I have done about it and how I feel. I found a little saying I'm going to follow. It's a paraphrase of something that Edward Everett Hale wrote. I've written it out and put it on my kitchen wall. It goes like this:

I am only one,
But I am one.
I can't do everything,
But I can do something.
And by the Grace of God,
What I *can* do, I *will* do!"

That conversation took place some time ago. My friend Pat still is sailing on an even keel. She bubbles over with joy and happiness and good cheer everywhere she goes.

If you would like to meet her sometime, drop by her church any Sunday morning. You will find her shoulder to shoulder with her friends in the choir, doing what she *can* do.

Lord, Don't Take Away
My Chariot Wheels

"Hey, Mom, lookee, lookee, here comes that chariot now!"

Everyone was still laughing at the child's remark as the big red, white, and blue bus spun into the parking lot of the church on Main Street.

It was not a chariot at all, at least not what we think of as a chariot. It was the bus that carries Ed and Bette Stalnecker and their Christian Crusade Team from one end of the United States to the other.

The little girl who cried out had been brought to the church to see the arrival of the Stalneckers. She had heard of the beautiful chariot that Pharaoh gave to Joseph when he made him ruler over all the land of Egypt. She related the colorful bus of the Stalneckers to the chariot in her Sunday-school lesson.

The children were fascinated as they watched the Crusade Team unload their trailer. First came the piano, then the organ, then the puppets and other equipment that traveled behind the bus.

My parents and the parents of Ed Stalnecker had

41

been close friends and neighbors when we were children. Our fathers worked together until his dad was transferred to Baton Rouge. More than twenty-five years had passed since I had seen Ed, and I was looking forward to seeing him again and meeting his family.

We were invited to visit their richly red-carpeted quarters, which they shared with the family pets—two dogs! "No matter how lovely this bus is," I thought out loud, "what would it be like to live on wheels 365 days a year?"

Ed was amused by my remark. "Because God has called me to do this particular work," he said, "he has given me the grace to adjust. I know this work. Therefore, I am secure." He anticipated my next question, saying, "I am not an evangelist or a revivalist. I am a church doctor. Within twenty-four hours I can diagnose the problem in any church."

We entered the church for the service. For the next hour we experienced an unforgettable blessing.

Bette, a contralto, lifted the hearts of everyone as she gave her testimony in song. She urged everyone to "place the broken pieces of your lives at the Savior's feet!" As she sang in sign language, for the benefit of the deaf, her song became like poetry in motion. That evening I learned that "applause" means "praise the Lord" in sign language. I often wish Christians did not refrain from applause during church services.

As Ed approached the altar to deliver the evening message, I saw a man who stood secure in the knowledge that he was doing exactly what the Lord wanted him to do. He reflected a life enmeshed in joy—a joy that drives him to heal the ills that infect the churches of America.

Their day-to-day personal sacrifices must be tremendous as they live in their home on wheels. Yet the Stalneckers keep rolling along from town to town, from church to church, from challenge to challenge.

I sometimes find it difficult to meet situations that are not nearly so trying. When I get so busy and become so frustrated that I feel that the wheels on my own chariot are spinning in the sand, I think of what Ed Stalnecker said.

Somehow I always manage to get my bus back on the highway and in high gear by asking God to "give me the grace to adjust."

Come Along with Me

If you ever have a chance, take a walk with an artist, a writer, or a composer. You'll find the experience refreshing, and might discover a whole new appreciation for a world you always have taken for granted.

My new world was opened for me by Ann Daniel Adams, the well-known southern accordionist and songwriter, on our first walk together. We both were guests of a convention group at a beach-side hotel on the Gulf Coast of Florida. At dinner I asked her how she found the inspiration for the songs she wrote.

"Let's take a walk on the beach after dinner and I'll show you," she said.

It was summer, and because of daylight saving time, we found ourselves headed for the beach just before sundown.

"Take off your shoes," she instructed. "The only way to walk on the beach is bare-footed."

As we headed up the beach, she said, "Now let me explain what happens when you seek communion with the out-of-doors. You must be aware of everything

44

going on around you. You must let nature reach you
through all of your senses. Stop now and look at the sun
as it drops below the horizon. That big red ball of fire.
See how it colors the clouds, not just around it, but
across the top of the sky and clear to the east behind
you. Look how the seagrass on the dunes seems to bow
and wave and say good-night to its dear friend as he
slips out of sight. Now turn and see how the shadows
of the palms are suddenly stretched clear up the side of
the hotel farther down the beach and across the golf
course beyond. Watch that bright red path that stretches
between you and the setting sun across the water. No
matter where you stand, that path leads directly from
you to the sun. But look quickly, it will be gone in a
minute."

"I never saw so many different things in one sun-
set," I said.

"Oh," Ann exclaimed, "you could look all night.
Everything changes every minute. But you must not
pamper your sense of sight. You must share the evening
with your ears. Listen. Hear the surf? Do you catch the
rhythm? It's steady, as though the orchestra leader has
selected the beat. He may change it if the wind asks him
to, but once he sets it, he finishes his tune. And the
gulls. Hear their good-night cry. And again, the seagrass.
Can't you hear it? Not loud and dominant as the break-
ing waves, but whispering and cooing as it rubs itself
down for a quiet night. There are a dozen noises, if you
will listen for them, each one playing its part in a big
outdoor ensemble.

"But there is more," she continued. "What about
your sense of smell? The salt air. Smell it? Taste it? How
pure! Blowing to us from across a thousand miles of
water. Not like the air of the dining room with its

human-made odors of food and cigarettes and hair oil. And don't forget the sense of feel. That's why we took off our shoes. Feel the sand and water between your toes? Now, let's walk."

So we did. For half an hour up and half an hour back, we walked without a word spoken. You notice that I did not say we walked "in silence."

No! We walked to the accompaniment of a heavenly orchestra. Ann hummed and whispered a gentle sort of lullaby. The surf furnished the bass and the beat. Our toes, squeaking through the sand, added an accent in the treble. Even my breathing became a part of this dreamy nocturne. As we approached our hotel and the cosmic stage lights dimmed, the closing crescendo reached our ears—a blend of the sea roar, the rumble of a far-off thunderstorm, the scream of an angry gull, and the whine of a huge passenger jet rising into the night.

As we said our good-nights and promised to meet for another walk on the beach before breakfast the next morning, I knew my question had been answered. I knew how Ann Daniel Adams found inspiration for the songs and lyrics that had made her a national celebrity. But I discovered more than that. I knew now why she had been the runner-up for Miss America in 1955, why she had been named the Florida Citrus Queen and the Radio Queen of the South, and why all of her other honors had come to her. I knew why her song, "Here Is Your Crown," is played at beauty pageants across our land.

She was in tune. That was it. She was a part of the celestial symphony!

Later, when I was ready for bed, I stepped onto the balcony of my tenth-floor room for a final look across the Gulf. The stars were shining now, and the soft wind that brushed my cheek was warm and carried a faint suggestion of night-blooming jasmine. Far below, the tempo of the waves against the beach had slowed, and their murmur seemed sleepier than before. As I stood there, I thought about my friend and what she had said about her source of inspiration. I thought, too, of another time and place and of another poet whose inspiration had come from the hand of the Great Creator.

His name was Isaiah, and he described his surroundings, and their promise: "For ye shall go out with joy, and be led forth with peace; the mountains and the hills shall break forth before you into singing, and all the trees of the field shall clap their hands."

Yes, Ann Daniel Adams had shared her world with me, and I was grateful. She had opened the door and invited me in, and I had entered.

The Graham Cracker Crowd

Children love to talk about their own names. Just as they can be hilariously funny when they are playing, they can be intensely serious when they discuss the names their mothers and fathers gave them. Just as we experience joy in seeing children's eagerness toward life, we also see behind their facade when they talk about their names.

Your name is emblazoned on you for a lifetime. It should be worn with pride and guarded with care. Psychologists say that our life can be warped or bruised by an unsuitable name or even thoughtless jesting about our name.

Once during the weekly story hour at our church library I asked the children, "Do you like your name?" Their responses came earnestly and without hesitation.

"The reason I like my name is it is almost my father's name. My name is Bobby. His name is Robert." Someday his friends will call him Bob.

"Mary Lynne is my name. I like the name. But you must know, it was not Mary Lynne until my mother

48

and father named it to me." I wonder what it was before.

"I love my name. It is Heather. Please call me Henny." She loves it, but not much.

"I wish so much that my name was Priscilla. It is my favorite movie star's wife's mother's name." She was so busy with the family tree, she forgot to tell us her own name.

"Michael is a pretty name for a boy. Everyone knows it is the prettiest name for a boy. So they just call me Michael." A good reason, don't you think?

"No, I do not like my name. It is Courtney. I would like to be named Ice because it is short." Cold, too.

"I wish my name was Wes. It is my favorite name. It is a good name for a boy. My name is Shirley. That's a girl's name and I hate it." I agree with that little boy. It isn't a good name for a football player.

"My name is just plain Sue. I wish it was Hildegarde Francene. That was my sister's name. She died. She is nine now." And still living in Sue's heart.

"My name is Paul and I like it because it cannot be changed." Here is a no-nonsense fellow.

"Sarah is my name. I hate it because I was named after my aunt." Do you suppose dear Aunt Sarah just changed her will?

"My name is Kenny Smith. I like it because I like to draw K's. I like it, too, because God made all the Smiths." The Smiths will be glad to hear that.

"My name is Cheryl. I used to not like my name, because I felt it was not very important. But everyone says it is an important name and so now I love my name." Her ego has been fed.

"Jeff is my name and it is a good name for a kid. When I am grown up I will change it, though." To Jefferson, no doubt.

"I wish my name was Jesus," said a little girl, "because nobody ever laughs at the name of Jesus. People laugh at my name, so I am not going to tell you what it is."

Someday when this little girl is an adult, she will be saddened to learn that there are people who do laugh at the name of Jesus. She will discover that the name of Jesus is often scorned and ridiculed.

You most often name a child for someone you love.

If you should be asked the names of the people in the Bible that you love the most, whom would you name? Possibly you would list Paul, Timothy, Moses, or Esther.

If you should be asked the names of the worst villains of the Bible, whom would you select? Would you put on this roll Judas, Herod, Cain, or Jezebel?

A familiar song tells us, "Jesus, Jesus, Jesus—there's just something about that name."

Jesus. The most beautiful name of all. Our Lord, Our Savior, Our Redeemer, Our Friend. And when you entrust your life to him, he permits you to bear his name—Christian.

Do you like your name?

I like mine.

But most of all I like to be called Christian.

Reaching Is Reaching
Is Reaching

Gene Shalit, movie and book critic for NBC, had just completed an interview with an author on the "Today" show. He was trying to push his way through the crowd gathered outside the television studio when a young businessman stepped up to him. "Mr. Shalit, would you please autograph my newspaper for me? I don't have a notepad or anything else. You see, Mr. Shalit, you have brought a bit of culture to my backwoods of Pennsylvania, and for that I am so grateful to you!"

Gene Shalit reached out for the gentleman's newspaper, autographed it, looked at him with a whimsical grin, and said, "And I am grateful to you for asking me."

Gene had invited a mutual friend and me to breakfast. After shaking half a dozen hands and signing a few autograph books, he led us down the escalator at the New York Hilton to the dining room. Still thinking about the man who had asked him to sign his newspaper, Gene said, "You know, it's the people you least expect that reach out to you and make the hustle and

51

bustle of this business all worthwhile. Asking me to sign
his newspaper was like a gift. Now I have received my
gift for today."

He seemed truly grateful, and I know that his gratitude and gentleness were felt by the young businessman,
and that he, too, had received his gift for the day.

Suddenly I saw that gift giving and gift receiving
really become gift sharing, because one has no value
without the other.

Whenever I think about that breakfast with Gene
Shalit, I am reminded of a painting in my den. The picture shows two hands. One is a tight-fisted chubby little
child's hand, clutching a bouquet of wild flowers. The
other is that of a woman, wide-stretched, reaching for
the blossoms that the child had picked. There would
have been no joy for the child if the hand of his friend
had not met his and accepted his precious gift.

Both hands are reaching out. Sharing their joy!

One of my favorite Bible stories tells about the
woman who reached out to Jesus. She had been ill for
twelve years, so the account goes, and she had joined
the multitudes seeking to be healed by the Master. Jesus
was hurrying through the crowd with Jairus, the leader
of the local synagogue, who had pleaded with him to
heal his little daughter. The press of people was so great
that the weak and feeble woman was unable to stand in
the forefront. With great effort and strain, she reached
toward Jesus as he rushed past. As he went by, the tips
of her fingers touched his cloak—and immediately she
was healed. A miracle!

The man who spoke to Gene Shalit, the lady who
accepted the child's gift, the woman who experienced
the miracle of healing—each had reached out.

On my flight home from New York and my visit to

the NBC studios, I thought about these three events. And there, thirty thousand feet in the sky, I realized for certain that nothing really happens for good in this world until you . . . reach out.

Cuddle Up a Little, Honey

"Book lady, please read me just one more story!"

This familiar plea always reminds me of how much I liked to have a book read to me when I was a child.

As director of our church library, I am called "book lady," a term I cherish, by many children. Our staff librarians spend hours reading books to groups of children. I have never found a child who did not beg us to read "just one more story."

There is an art to getting children interested in books and stories. You must LOVE them into reading! You have to stimulate their imagination. Use pictures, music, puppets, or even real animals. Help them picture what you are reading about in the stories.

One morning I had a restless little boy who was determined that he was going out on the playground rather than listen to the stories. Because I was reading a story about a little wild squirrel, one of the teachers had brought to the library a live gray squirrel in a cage. The children were invited to feed the squirrel with a tiny

doll's bottle while I read the story. The restless youngster was the first to feed the squirrel. Immediately he
became interested and began to ask questions about
squirrels and where they lived.

When the storytelling hour was over and the children were pleading with me to read "just one more
story," the little fellow said, "Book lady, I liked the
squirrel in the book lots better than the one in the
cage!"

Right then I learned a lesson about reading to children. The loving and coaxing must always precede the
telling.

Eve Titus, a gifted author who has written dozens of
books about the little French mouse, Anatole, taught
me another lesson. She showed me how to use imagina
tion and love in teaching children to appreciate books
and to want to read. Mrs. Titus was on crutches, re-
cuperating from a broken leg, when she and I met and
chatted at a book fair. "Writing a book is a lovely thing
to do, but you have to have imagination," she said.
"However, imagination alone is not enough. You must
include the element of love, or you will end up with
nothing."

A news story was published recently reporting on a
study made by twenty top educators. They spent three
years on the project and assembled data from 1,807
schools. They reached the following conclusion: "The
best way to prepare the very young child for reading is
to hold him on your lap and read aloud to him stories
he likes—over and over again."

Wouldn't our grandparents and our parents laugh
at this report? Their natural instinct told them to
take us in their laps and teach us the joy hidden in
books. Everyone knows that love is the world's great

motivator. Love of reading emphasizes that eternal truth.

Jesus was the first to teach this lesson when he said, "Suffer the little children to come unto me. . . ."

The world does not need a panel of educators to tell us what love can do—even for a child. Jesus did that nearly two thousand years ago.

So you see, the book or story is important—but it's the cuddle that really counts.

Me? A Pelican?

The woodcarver caressed a small block of cypress and began to chisel away this piece and that. In a few minutes he had finished a tiny replica of a brown pelican.

His work fascinated me, and when he had made his final cut, I spoke to him. "I notice that you do not work from a pattern or a sketch or a picture. How can you begin to cut away the wood without a design to follow?"

The old gentleman smiled broadly at me. "Lady, do you know what you are to become?" He did not wait for an answer. "No, you do not. But the Great Creator does. He can shape you into what he wants you to be, if you are willing. This piece of wood is willing. It does not prevent me from making it into whatever I feel in my heart, or letting my knife go where it is guided. I can see what I want it to be before I touch my knife to it."

Needless to say, I bought that little wooden pelican. It brought joy to my life, because of the craftsman's words.

It rests on my desk, posing the challenge: Am I willing?

Another bird, much larger, also brings back stimulating thoughts.

I shall never forget the morning my husband and I were on hand to witness the launching of the manned spaceship Gemini 5—August 21, 1965. There stood the ten-story-high silver bird, breathing out tiny wisps of vapor, waiting for the countdown.

Sitting in the nose were astronauts L. Gordon Cooper, Jr., and Charles Conrad, Jr., who would ride in their tiny module for eight days. Nearly a million people were there. They were scattered for miles up and down the Florida coast, in cars or campers, on bicycles or afoot. All eyes looked to the shiny rocket that seemed so small against the horizon. We were told it was five miles from where we stood.

Thousands of portable radios kept the crowds aware of the pending lift-off as the seconds ticked away.

Then, ". . . three, two, one. We have ignition. We have lift-off."

And with the fire and smoke and roar from the silver bird came a flood of tears.

As I stood there trembling, awed, a bit frightened and overwhelmed by man's accomplishment, a thought took shape. This bird was like the pelican on my desk. Like the hands of the man who worked with his willing piece of cypress, the steady hands of a thousand men or more had worked with a million willing bits and pieces of cloth and wood and metal to shape this rocket. And in their vision they saw man someday walking on the moon.

I remembered what the man said as he cut away the chips of cypress: "The Great Creator can shape you into what he wants you to be, if you are willing."

If the woodcarver with only a knife and a block of cypress and his limited skill can create a little pelican, and if space scientists with their restricted knowledge can hurl a rocket to the moon, think how much more God Almighty can do with you with all of his unlimited power and wisdom—if you are willing.

Jesus calls on you to exercise faith. Faith as a wee grain of mustard seed is all you need.

Faith in the Creator is willingness to be clay in the potter's hands—faith in His vision of what he wants you to become.

When you are truly willing, and when you put your self in His hands, the supreme woodcarver will shape you into a masterpiece.

Me? A pelican? Not really.

I don't care what God shapes me into as long as he says, when finished, "This is my child, in whom I am well pleased."

God's Point of View

As Ellen de Kroon hobbled into the dining room on crutches and took her place at the breakfast table, she declared, "I'm certainly not hypocrite enough to say I'm glad I broke my ankle. But since I did break it, I'm glad I did it while I was here."

I felt the same way.

Here was a case of a broken ankle bringing me great happiness. Not because she broke her ankle, but because she would now be staying with us for at least three weeks, instead of three days. Ellen works as secretary and companion to Miss Corrie ten Boom. The joy of having both Ellen and Corrie with us for three weeks was almost more than I could believe.

Corrie ten Boom captured my heart even before I had finished reading the book about her life, *The Hiding Place*, written by John and Elizabeth Sherrill. The Sherrills tell the story of the ten Booms, a Christian family living in Haarlem in the Netherlands. They operated a watchmaker's shop in their home. In 1940, when the Nazis occupied their country, the ten Booms' house became "the hiding place" for many Jewish refugees. The little watchmaker's place served as an important underground stop in the Jewish escape route.

The ten Booms' involvement in the plight of the Jews began rather casually. One Sunday evening a friend of theirs, a Jewish neighbor, asked if she could stay overnight, because the Nazis were coming to arrest her. They let her stay, and the next day she made her way into the countryside, where an escape network was in operation.

A few days later three Jewish youths showed up in the same dilemma, and the ten Booms helped them. Before long a steady stream of frightened Jewish neighbors were asking for protection while waiting for the escape organization to slip them out of Holland.

Then one day a mystery man showed up. Years later Corrie learned that he was one of the most famous architects in Europe. He had come to rip out and rebuild and remodel. When he left a week later, a tiny secret closet, "the hiding place," had been squeezed behind a 150-year-old wall.

The ten Booms were no longer helping casually. Their commitment had become total.

Corrie and her sister, Betsie, and their father were eventually caught by the Germans and sent to a concentration camp.

The Hiding Place describes Corrie's stay there. It shows how the death of her father and sister, while in confinement, put her faith to the supreme test and taught her a new meaning of Christian forgiveness.

And now she was a guest in our home.

Corrie loved the warm Florida sunshine. One morning she and Ellen and several of my friends had gathered to enjoy breakfast in our garden. "Tante" Corrie, as her friends affectionately call her, spoke in a soft voice to bring us many of her pithy words of faith and witness.

"When God is second," she said, "you will come out second best, but when God is really first, you will always come out first. Your life can be like a ribbon between your God and you. And when God has called you, do not spend time looking over your shoulder to see who is following. All of you, look around and be distressed, look within and be depressed, look to Jesus and be at rest—and God will make your home a hiding place."

She paused for a moment, then continued, "I know that the experiences of our lives, when we let God use them, become the mysterious and perfect preparation for the work he will give us to do."

After a while she reached for the hands of the persons seated on either side of her, and without a spoken word we formed a prayer circle.

Tante Corrie then asked God to come into her heart and make her a tool to do his work that day. She spoke to God in simple terms. She told him her problems while we listened. The conversation seemed almost as though it were a two-way communication, as though Corrie were discussing her plans for the day with a close friend. Her prayer ended with a Dutch-sounding "Aamen and Aamen." Then, with a silent nod, she broke the circle and went into the house to begin work on a speech she would deliver that evening.

Ellen stayed with us a while longer. One of our guests asked her, "Tante Corrie has a constant communication line open with Jesus, doesn't she?"

"Ya," she replied. "That is the inspiring part about being with Tante Corrie. She teaches me to look at things from God's point of view, to look at God's pattern, to talk everything over with him—even the smallest problems."

What did she say? "God's point of view"? I had never thought of that. I had always approached problem solving from my own point of view.

It's true that I daily repeated the old standby phrase, "Thy will be done." But now I would say, "Dear Lord, let me look at this situation from your point of view."

During her stay, Tante Corrie encouraged us to talk to God about everything, no matter how trivial.

"He is your loving Father," she reminded us. "He sees your problems before you even know they are there. Prayer is not so much asking God to take over your affairs as it is attuning yourself with his will, establishing a closeness with him, letting him help you work out your daily problems together."

Corrie ten Boom's wisdom. God's point of view.

Pass the Peanut Butter

"Tell me how to make a peanut butter and jelly sandwich. That will be your first assignment in creative writing," Professor Ginger Allsopp announced to her class on the opening day of school.

The students tittered with amusement. "Imagine college students getting such a ridiculous assignment," one husky football player said when the class was over.

The following week, after the papers had been carefully checked, Mrs. Allsopp reported to the class, "Not a single one tells me exactly what to do. I will read you one of them and will follow the instructions as I read."

She set a loaf of bread, a jar of peanut butter, and a crock of jelly on her desk as she read. "Take two slices of bread. Put peanut butter on one slice and jelly on the other slice. Now your sandwich is ready to eat." She then placed two slices of bread on her desk. On one slice she set the jar of peanut butter. On the other slice she set the crock of jelly. Then she raised her head and stared at the class with a quizzical look.

Immediately the students began to laugh at their

64

own stupidity. Professor Allsopp had made her point. Clarity is the most important contribution to understanding.

Mrs. Allsopp pointed out that clarity and simplicity go hand in hand. "For example," she said, "take the great author-naturalist Henry David Thoreau. He spoke and wrote in such unaffected language that anyone could understand him. He was a master of easy teaching and learning. Remember what he said: 'Our life is frittered away by detail . . . simplify, simplify.' "

A perfect example of clarity and simplicity in speaking comes from the Master Teacher, Jesus. He taught in clear, simple parables. Everyone who heard him understood—the educated pharisees, the unlearned fishermen, the illiterate nomads of the desert, even the children.

The message was clear to all of them when Jesus told the story of the mustard seed to show how the Kingdom of God grows and increases, when he told them about the prodigal son to illustrate the love and forgiveness of God the Father, when he used the parable of the talents to explain that God expected them to use what He had given them, and when he told them about the good Samaritan to show that we cannot love God unless we love people.

Parables can increase our perception and help us find answers.

The parables of Jesus. Perhaps a parable you might write. Or Professor Allsopp's parable of the peanut butter and jelly sandwich.

How Good It Is

P.S. How good it is to see each of these men—
Howard Butt, Mike Douglas, Hans G. Tanzler, Jr., and
Jack Nicklaus—in totally unrelated worlds, spreading
joy every day, wherever they go.
                              The End
                         ————

Oh, I know you never add a "P.S." to a manuscript
until you have completed it, and then only as an after-
thought. But I became so excited as I recalled the inci-
dents I had witnessed firsthand in the lives of these men
that I wanted to tell you about them—from the end
back to the beginning.

Jack Nicklaus, the "Golden Bear" of professional
golf, has been called the world's greatest golfer. I am a
fan of his. So is his family. Jack's wife, Barbara, and
their children follow him on his rounds whenever they
can. Once when he was playing for the PGA champion-
ship, he missed winning by only one stroke. As he
putted out on the final green, he knew he had come in
second. When he removed his ball from the cup and

66

straightened up, in this moment of great disappointment, he saw his wife and son, Gary, standing on the edge of the huge crowd.

While television cameras ground away and sportscasters thrust microphones toward him and fans clamored for his autograph, Jack ignored them. With a solemn visage, trying to mask his distress, he walked to the spot where his wife and little boy were standing. He leaned over, picked up Gary, raised him to his shoulder, then turned back toward the crowd. In that instant, his look of despair had turned into the famous Jack Nicklaus smile. And everyone knew he was taking his defeat like a true champion. He already was thinking about the next tournament and how he was planning to win it.

Hans G. Tanzler, Jr., mayor of Jacksonville, Florida, is plagued with the usual problems that concern every other mayor of a large city—law and order, fire protection, schools, streets and highways, sewers, taxes, money, and on and on. My husband, Dexter, frequently meets with him, either to talk business or play golf. Once after a business conference with Hans, Dexter said to me, "I don't see how he stands the tension and pressure that he must be under. He's always so calm and cool and collected. Nothing ever seems to ruffle him."

Several days later, Dexter received a letter from him discussing their recent meeting. As though he were reading the question on Dexter's mind, he closed with these words: "Needless to say, my recent religious experience has completely changed my outlook toward people and life and made it possible for me to carry my heavy burden of responsibility because now it is shared by our Lord and Savior."

Mike Douglas always seems utterly composed and in command when he comes into your living room via television. Yet I once saw behind his facade. I saw him "carry on" and perform under circumstances that might well have crushed a man of lesser physical and emotional stamina.

He had come to Florida to produce his show in the magnificent setting of Cypress Gardens. At the time, I was serving as the coordinator between his staff and the office of the Florida Citrus Showcase. For several weeks I worked side by side with them during their rigorous taping schedule. About halfway through the series, Mike received the news that a member of his immediate family had been rushed to the hospital and was not expected to live.

"I've got to go," he told me. "I should be there every day until we're sure he'll pull through."

And he was.

Every afternoon when the taping session was over, Mike drove eighty-five miles to the Tampa airport, caught the evening plane, and flew to the bedside where he felt he belonged. In the early hours of the morning, he flew back to Tampa, retraced those weary miles to Cypress Gardens, and stepped onto the television set promptly at nine o'clock.

Not once did he complain about being tired. Not once did he ask for any special consideration. Even when he was almost out on his feet, he worked with as much gusto as anyone else on the set. And as you watched him that day on the screen in your home, he looked and acted like a man who didn't have a care in the world—a man who had enjoyed eight hours of worry-free sleep the night before.

Howard Butt stood at the crossroads of two possible careers. Would he remain in the grocery business, where he had been working successfully for fifteen years, or would he follow his lay ministry, which was then demanding about one-third of his time?

His decision was imminent because his father, the founder of the largest independent food chain in Corpus Christi and for whom Howard worked, was retiring. The top spot in the business would go to either Howard or his younger brother. His brother had said pointedly that if Howard were named head of the company, he would have to give up his preaching and devote full time to the business or else he would have to run it alone. His brother told Howard that he would not work for a part-time minister/part-time groceryman. He also said he would like to be the general manager himself, and if he were given the job, he would work at it eagerly, enthusiastically—and full time.

In a book titled *The Velvet Covered Brick*, Howard Butt tells about this confrontation and why he turned his back on the business world. He explains why he chose to direct his interdenominational ministries through the Laity Lodge Foundation rather than pursue a business career that promised to make him a millionaire.

Our paths crossed when I received a copy of his book for review on my television show. In it he talks about authority and submission and the importance of being able to accept authority gracefully. "If you are a revolutionary," he says, "you cannot change the Establishment. If you are a leader, you cannot change the revolutionaries. You can change no one but yourself."

Four men. Four lives. Four examples.

A Pocketful of Miracles

When Artur Rubinstein was asked the secret of his success, he explained, "I have adopted the technique of living life from miracle to miracle." Those who have heard the famous pianist play know the full depth of a Rubinstein miracle.

Miracles happen around us every day, in your life, in mine. The Scriptures refer to miracles as "marvelous things" and "marvelous works" and as signs and wonders performed through the power of God. However, we sometimes fail to recognize a miracle when it occurs in our own back yard. Only a truly humble person will admit that the miracle came from God and was not of his own doing. Genuine gratitude is expressed when we thank God for our miracles and praise him for his goodness.

Miracles make life exciting. They are gifts that have been promised by God to his children. Why don't you claim this promise? Ask for miracles, and when they come, be grateful.

What miracles have you experienced in your life? Ask yourself that question. Your answer might surprise

you. Certainly it will be revealing. The closer you stand
to God, the more miracles you will find, the more happenings you will perceive as coming from his hand.

When I think of miracles, I think of Dr. John Eger
Howard, of Johns Hopkins University Hospital, a true
miracle-worker.

Dr. Howard stands tall in the medical world. His
study of hypoglycemia (low blood-sugar) has earned
him a permanent place in medical reference books. As
important to him as his skill in medicine is his Christian
faith. With humility and modesty, he gives God credit
for his success.

Every day God hands Dr. Howard a new miracle. He
helps him pinpoint the causes of rare diseases. He looks
over his shoulder as he performs his diagnostic examina-
tions on the hundreds of patients who come to the
clinic every week. Even though Dr. Howard is advancing
in years, God keeps giving him the strength to work
marathon hours.

I am sure that if you asked this distinguished physi-
cian about the miracles in his life, he would be surprised
that you had noticed. Like Rubinstein, he lives and
works from miracle to miracle.

One of those miracles saved my sister's life.

It was the Christmas season. Janet had been gravely
ill for two weeks. Finally, in a coma, she was moved by
ambulance-train from Florida to Baltimore. Three
nurses looked after her around the clock.

After a long delay because of a blizzard, the train
pulled into the Baltimore station hours behind schedule.
Janet was close to death. This had to be the gloomiest,
dreariest, unhappiest Christmas Day I had ever known.

You can imagine our concern. Would the doctor
come to the hospital on Christmas Day? Would he be

able to diagnose Janet's problem and begin treatment right away? Would the ambulance be waiting for us after this long delay?

The Lord said, "Yes."

The ambulance was there. And Dr. Howard was at the hospital. He not only was taking care of his patients that day, but was prepared and standing by for my sister's arrival. In his long black overcoat, he rushed into the sleet and snow to help the ambulance attendants roll Janet into the hospital on her stretcher.

Then a miracle began to unfold.

Within a few hours, Dr. Howard was able to diagnose the illness and begin treatment. Before the night was over, we felt relief that we had her under his care. Within a few weeks, we could see my sister take a turn for the better. Although we knew her recovery would be slow, we knew, with no doubts, that it would be certain.

When Dr. Howard was asked how he discovered the cause of her illness and decided on the proper treatment, he silently pointed his finger toward the heavens. He may have been thinking of the great Ambroise Pare's answer when asked the same question: "I dressed his wounds and God healed him."

More than seventy-five years ago, Fanny Crosby wrote these words that are still sung in our churches: "To God be the Glory, great things he hath done."

Including a multitude of miracles.

Hair Plastered
With Grape Jelly

"My idea of a perfect day is when all three of my babies have slept a full night, when the toilet has not run over, and when I only have one more washer-load of diapers to do," said a neighbor of mine. "Oh, yes, and when I can get away to the store without grape jelly in my hair."

What is your idea of a perfect day?

Would it be a day at your typewriter, uninterrupted? Would it be a day at the beach and a swim in the ocean? Would it be a day when you could invite friends over to share a moment of joy?

My pastor's wife, Wanda Gamble, says that a perfect day for her begins with a definite appointment with God. She keeps her appointment every morning between 7:00 and 7:45 A.M. "It was ten years ago," she said, "that I learned I needed to have a definite appointment to talk to God. I needed him to help me plan my day. I could not take the chance that I would find the time later on. I never take a chance on getting an appointment at the beauty parlor, or at the doctor's office, or with the dentist. I always have a definite time to go. Just so with God. My appointment begins my day. And any day that begins with God has to be a perfect day."

Aren't we wrong to blame God when our day turns out less than perfect? Especially if we did not even talk to him about it?

Almost every day when I go to the post office, I meet a certain elderly little man who suffers from an incurable and painful ailment. "How are you today?" I ask. And he always answers, "If it gets any gooder, I don't know if I can stand it." I always feel better and often go away whistling just because of the sunshine he adds to my day.

Every day has its flat tires and weak batteries and bumpy roads, but our ride becomes smoother when we begin the journey with a quiet time of prayer. Anyone can make a prayer appointment. The time of day is not important. Making and keeping the appointment are.

And so, from my pastor's wife and the little man in the post office, I have developed a formula for my own perfect day. It begins with a prayer appointment with God. And it always includes a conscious effort to help someone else have a perfect day.

There are so many ways you can help make a perfect day for others.

You can listen with excited curiosity instead of a shrug of indifference.

You can show sincere delight over their successes instead of wallowing in jealousy.

You can exclaim over something of beauty rather than comment on an unhappy thought.

You can exhibit trust and faith in them instead of planting a seed of doubt or suspicion.

How can you have a perfect day?

You don't need to listen to the lady with grape jelly in her hair or a little man in your post office. All you need to do is make your daily appointment with God and heed the words of Jesus when he says, "Ask and it shall be given you; seek and ye shall find; knock and it shall be opened unto you."

And remember, when you ask, seek, and knock, be sure you include helping someone else have a happy day too.

It's the Real Thing!

Joe Garagiola, broadcasting a baseball game between the Pittsburgh Pirates and the Cincinnati Reds, quipped that he agreed with his friend who observed, "I dunno about this artificial turf. Personally, I don't want to play on any grass a horse can't eat!"

Today we find artificial turf on baseball diamonds, football fields, golf putting greens, and other places where natural grass should be growing.

Artificial. Substitute. Duplicate. Imitation. All about us we see people working in experimental laboratories copying everything from emeralds to sugar.

One morning in a restaurant, I overheard a big, burly truckdriver saying that he had been served "a disgusting substitute" for bacon, eggs, and milk. "What happened to pig's bacon, hen's eggs, and cow's milk?" he demanded.

Substitutes for many things can be born in test tubes. Man constantly strives to create. And he has been able to invent and manufacture all sorts of clever substitutes for all sorts of natural products.

He has even figured a way to imitate laughter. He can splice it onto tape to help put us in a happy mood when we watch television or listen to the radio.

But he can't duplicate everything.

This was once brought home to me following an extended rehearsal in a television studio. My eyes had been severely burned by high-intensity lights, and I was taken to the hospital. Dr. Howard Lucas, an ophthalmologist, was called to the emergency room to examine me. "The best medicine for your eyes now will be tears," he informed me. "They lubricate and heal like no other medicine. No scientist or doctor ever has been able to reproduce the exact formula of a tear."

Neither has he developed a substitute for love. Especially the love of Jesus Christ—the only medicine that can cure a sick or suffering soul.

Paul said, "Love is patient and kind; love is not jealous or boastful; it is not arrogant or rude. Love does not insist on its own way; it is not irritable or resentful; it does not rejoice at wrong, but rejoices in the right.

"Love bears all things, believes all things, hopes all things, endures all things.

"Love never ends."

Who would be vain enough to try to invent a substitute for that?

Who would want to accept anything other than . . . the real thing!

Would You Choose You?

Recently I sat in church behind a man who was wearing a red suit. It was redder than a cardinal or an apple or even a poppy. As I watched, it seemed to grow redder and redder. I kept thinking that he looked like a huge fire-extinguisher. I wondered whether his wife had bought it for him so he could play Santa at Christmas time or whether he had been double-crossed by his tailor.

I was so intent on wondering why he would wear such a colorful suit to church that I was not aware that he had stepped into the aisle and walked to the grand piano. Suddenly he was playing the most beautiful music I had ever heard. That man! The man wearing the gaudy red suit was the pianist I had come to hear, the star performer of the evening—a man with a great talent. I was embarrassed when I realized I had been so critical of his dress that I almost missed the joy of his music.

What a surprise, I thought. What unlikely people so often do the greatest work. Seldom are they the persons you would select.

Who would have chosen a gangly farm boy from the Piedmont region of North Carolina to become the best-known evangelist of our time? Yet, with the talent God gave him, Billy Graham has crossed denominational, ethnic, and national barriers to reach a wider audience than any other man living today. What a surprise he must be to his boyhood friends.

Who would have picked the twelve men that Jesus chose for his helpers? I don't think I would have. I would have said to Andrew, "Andrew, you come on too strong. Cool it. Don't be so pushy." But Jesus encouraged his zest and gave him an important job.

I hardly think I would have chosen Peter. I would have said, "Peter, you are hyperactive and impulsive. Sit down. Quit pacing the floor." But look how Jesus relied on him.

I would have been afraid of local gossip if I had asked Matthew (that unpopular tax collector) to join my group. Philip was too unimaginative and too slow to understand. Thomas was so overly cautious and such a negative thinker that I would have ignored him. And Judas, man of mystery, I don't know.

Did those men each have a valuable talent? Jesus thought so.

And what about you and me? Who would select one of us? Only someone overflowing with compassion, someone with a deep sense of understanding and a forgiving heart, someone who can see our hidden talents.

Yes, God has chosen each of us. Each has been given an assignment—and a talent to go with it. Just like the concert pianist in the red suit, the farm boy turned evangelist, or the odd assortment of men that Jesus chose.

My Dad Can Beat Your Dad

The introductions at the debutante ball had taken an odd turn. Instead of the usual custom of mentioning only the girls' parents, the master of ceremonies was adding bits and pieces about their other antecedents.

One young lady was presented as the great-granddaughter of a vice-president of the United States, another as a descendant of a famous college president, and one as the granddaughter of a great railroad tycoon. None lacked a distinguished name in her background.

The debutantes themselves may have been pleased with the performance, but to most of the audience, the lengthy genealogies had become ludicrous if not downright boring. The lady sitting on my right summed up her feelings by whispering to me, "Ancestors are like potato vines—the only part worth talking about is under ground." I recognized an old saying that I had heard from my dad all my life.

Nathaniel Hawthorne and Voltaire appeared to share the viewpoint of my neighbor, for they too

spoofed genealogical importance. Voltaire: "Who serves
his country well has no need of ancestors." Hawthorne:
"Once in every half century, at longest, a family should
be merged into the great, obscure mass of humanity and
forget all about its ancestors."

Yet there are some who try to bask in the reflected
light of their forebears. We see it even in the words of
the little boy who says, "My dad can beat your dad."
Someday, while he is dreaming that his dad will do his
fighting for him, some little nondreamer is going to give
him a punch in the nose.

The great French writer Lewis Galantiere expressed
the truth well when he wrote, "To be a man is, pre-
cisely, to be responsible." We must be responsible for
our own actions. As we will be held accountable for our
errors and failures, so will we be crowned for our tri-
umphs and successes. You never will receive the Nobel
Prize for a novel that your grandfather wrote. The world
says we must stand on our own feet.

That truth itself cries out in favor of education and
training.

I remember a visit to Baltimore and to my friends
Nancy and Bill Cochran. Bill owns an upholstery and
antique shop. He was talking about the scarcity of
trained craftsmen. "Unemployment? Listen, I've got
half a dozen jobs that are going begging. I can't find
skilled craftsmen. I need somebody who knows how
to cane a chair. The man who works for me is seventy-
two years old and wants to quit. I need somebody to
take his place. But in all of Baltimore I haven't been
able to find anybody who knows how to cane a chair.
And nobody knows how to refinish the fine old woods
in antique furniture, either. The worst part is—nobody wants to learn. Young people today are looking

for high-paying jobs that don't require any training."

Then he told me about the early training guilds in Europe and how they worked: "Each guild was headed by a master craftsman who taught apprentices a trade. The masters were jealous of their skills and set extremely high standards for their pupils. Once an apprentice had graduated, he could call himself a master craftsman and set up business for himself. Sometimes a master craftsman would become so famous that applicants had to wait as long as five years for an opportunity to serve as one of his apprentices. But not anymore. Nobody wants to learn. Everybody wants instant success. People don't want to stand on their own feet."

Stand on your own feet, said the master craftsmen of another day.

So said the Great Master. Once when he was talking to his disciples, he said, "You are the light of the world." Notice that he did not say, "Your father or grandfather or his father. . . ."

He said, "*You* are the light of the world. . . . Let your light so shine before men, that they may see your good works, and glorify your Father which is in heaven."

Give Me Patience
–But Hurry!

The shrilling siren, the flashing blue light, and the fact that I could see no other car on the street told me I was in trouble! The policeman climbed out of his patrol car and made his way to my vehicle. Before he could say a single word, I gave him ten excuses why I did not have time to be delayed. He listened and smiled politely. Then he wrote me one of those dreadful tickets.

Needless to say, I arrived late for my dental appointment and dashed into the waiting room, bumping headlong into a long-time family friend, Angela Wertz. Whenever I see Angela, I know I am going to get a sample of peppermint candy and a taste of homespun philosophy. Sure enough, she pulled a small candy cane out of her handbag and said, "My dear, my dear, it's okay to get in a flurry, but don't be in such a hurry!"

"That's my problem," I said. "Look." And I showed her the traffic ticket. "If I hadn't caught three red lights on Central Avenue and then had to wait at the park for the freight train, I wouldn't have been hurrying so."

83

"The dentist is running a little behind schedule," the nurse interrupted.

I sat down beside Angela to wait. She reached over and patted my hand. "See now, everything works out for the best," she assured me. "If the police had not stopped you, maybe you would have had an accident, speeding to get here."

Angela has stood by my side during many traumatic experiences. She always is able to calm me with her words of wisdom, plus the soothing effect of her peppermint candy.

"Well, I'm in trouble now," I told her. "It was impatience, pure and simple, that landed me in hot water."

Angela laughed, "Well, dear, I don't know of a better remedy for any trouble than old-fashioned patience."

I continued to chastise myself: "You can see that I did not heed my pastor's Sunday sermon. He said patience is better than pride, and through faith and patience we will inherit the promises of God. He pointed out that God is pleased when we exercise patience in all things. And here I am showing no patience in anything!"

"Patience is something you have to practice every day," Angela counseled. "You have learned an expensive lesson today. Maybe a thirty-five-dollar lesson. Whenever you think about it, you will be reminded to be patient. Longfellow wrote a few lines about patience that I memorized when I was a little girl: 'Though the mills of God grind slowly, yet they grind exceeding small; though with patience He stands waiting, with exactness grinds He all.'"

As I rushed home from the dentist's office, already late to prepare supper, I got behind an old truck that was barely moving in traffic. Exasperated because there was no way to pass the truck, I whispered a quick prayer: "God, please give me patience—but hurry!"

Then I laughed at myself as I saw one of Angela's red and white candy canes lying on the dashboard of my car. . . . a peppermint reminder to be patient.

The Fallen Arch

Hurtling through space at more than a hundred miles an hour, the man was kicking, flailing his arms, and fighting desperately as his parachute trailed unopened above him like a streamer against the blue summer sky. At first the crowd thought his fall was part of the sky-diving team's exhibition. But in moments they realized this was no well-rehearsed stunt. The jumper was in trouble, serious trouble. He catapulted toward the ground as hysterical screams from onlookers filled the atmosphere.

Arch Deal, a popular television anchorman and a veteran parachutist of more than fifteen hundred jumps, then crashed into a grove of citrus trees. He lay motionless, with his faulty parachute snagged in the uppermost branches of an orange tree. He had fallen three thousand feet. Yet he lived. He suffered serious but not permanent injuries.

I did not see Arch Deal fall, but I did visit him in the hospital afterward.

The newspaper headlines and the radio and tele-

86

vision announcements labeled his survival "a modern-day miracle." Indeed it was.

Moments before he had climbed into the plane to begin the exhibition jump, he remarked to friends, "With the mechanism in this new chute, there is no way it can malfunction. It is the surest, safest parachute made."

My friend Arch Deal was confident his parachute was infallible. He entrusted his life to his equipment. He was positive nothing could prevent a perfect jump and a safe landing. But something did. His rip cord failed to work properly. Then his lines became entangled.

Life, like a parachute, can give you an umbrella of protection. It can allow you to float wonderfully through to a safe landing, or it can malfunction and spell disaster. You must be confident of your equipment. Certainly! You must not be afraid of life. But you always should be prepared for trouble. If your rip cord of life should fail, you must be sure that the lines you hold do not become entangled.

Mrs. Paul Dilley and Tom Tichenor, both master puppeteers and teachers of the art, caution their students, "Your strings must never become entangled. But if they should, be sure you have a master plan."

And the Master does give you a plan to use when your strings become crossed. He said, "Come unto me, all ye that labor and are heavy laden, and I will give you rest." He knows that you will not always land safely. If you should fall, he promises to catch you and stand you back on your feet.

The man who trusts his life to a parachute must keep his lines clear, or his parachute is of no use. His whole being depends on the slender cords that connect him to that big canopy of billowy silk overhead.

And so it is with us—every day. Our joy and welfare and safety depend on the thin lines that connect us to our protection—the love and grace of God Almighty.

The skydiver calls his lines Nylon.

In our case, our lines are called Faith.

Formula for Face Wrinkles

"Are you fun to live with?"

This sign was pasted to the refrigerator door in the kitchen of a friend of mine. As we sat down to have a glass of iced tea, I was laughing at the question posed in bold red letters. "Carolyn, is that intended for any particular member of the family?" I teased.

"No," she replied. "It's for all of us. With two teen-age daughters in the house, sometimes we need a reminder that we not only have to consider other people, but we can have a good time doing it." Smiling, she added, "You would be amazed to know how much joy and understanding that sign has generated, especially when we read it at the beginning of the day."

I have thought about that sign many times.

So often a catchy little motto or wise saying can start our day in the right direction.

The Bible refers to those one-line sayings of wisdom as "seeds." Ecclesiastes examines life to help us find total satisfaction. This venerable book, written more than twenty-three hundred years ago, offers proof of the point that complete contentment can be found only in God. In those days there were no psychiatrists, psychologists, or mental-health clinics.

As I was waiting in a supermarket check-out line, an elderly woman with two bags of groceries stood in front of me. After she had paid her bill, she tucked a bag under each arm and began shuffling out the door. One of the bag boys rushed up to her and asked, "Ma'am, can I carry those to the car for you?"

"Thank you, young man," she said, "but I don't have a car. I'm walking, and I can manage."

The boy began untying his work apron. "Ma'am, I'm off for my supper hour now. Can I drive you home in my car?"

The tired lines in the old lady's face relaxed. She looked relieved. "Oh, thank you! It's nearly a mile to my house, and I'd have to sit a spell every once in a while and get my breath. Thank you, young man. I'll wait until you're ready."

The boy disappeared for a moment to put his apron in the back of the store.

Realizing that I had overheard the conversation, the woman turned to me and said, "Isn't that nice of him? But you know, I'm not surprised. This morning when I got up, I said to myself, 'Something good is going to happen to me today.' And it did."

Something good is going to happen to me today.

What an invigorating idea! What a refreshing little motto. Think how much joy it would create if it were pasted on your refrigerator door for you to see at the beginning of each day.

Thoughts of joy will do more than lift your mind and heart spiritually. They work as a cosmetic treatment. They relax your facial muscles, they erase your wrinkles, and they bathe your face with a glowing sheen.

Jesus believed in the power of wise sayings and proverbs. He left us with many thoughts that would stimulate your day from your refrigerator door. You might want to paste up a new one each month.

Why not try one of my favorites as a starter: "If ye have faith as a grain of mustard seed, ye shall say unto this mountain, remove hence to yonder place; and it shall remove; and nothing shall be impossible unto you."

Flip-flops or Cyclops

Cyclops, the ugly giant of Greek mythology who had one large eye in the center of his forehead, came to mind on my way to church one morning. The sermon title had been announced as "One-Eyed Christians."

"What a horrible thought," I told myself.

So it was not the message, but the messenger, that put joy in my step as I hurried to hear Dr. John Haggai of Atlanta. I had read Dr. Haggai's book, *How to Win over Worry*, and was curious to hear a man who claimed to have defeated the worry habit.

As he spoke that morning, I received far more than a lesson in curing the worry habit. I heard John Haggai call all of us to the task of being one-eyed Christians. He said each of us should concentrate on one particular job and purpose in the work of God.

Dr. Haggai himself stands as an example of this principle. He has funneled every ounce of his talent and strength toward building the program known as Haggai Institute for Advanced Leadership Training. Under this plan, key persons in countries around the world are selected and trained as Christian leaders. They then return home to continue the work of missions. The effectiveness of a man or woman working with his own people, in his own land, has been proved over and over. The bonds of Christian love and understanding that they build are strong and long-lasting.

"Under God," Dr. Haggai emphasized that morning, "those involved in Haggai Institute's program are committed to a single objective. We do not scatter our fire. . . . We simply do what we do best by investing our total energies, under God, in the one pursuit to which we have been divinely called." They no longer tend to become what he called "flip-flop" Christians.

Suddenly the message of Cyclops came through. Christians should follow the advice of Paul: Find the job in the Kingdom you are best suited for—and stick to it.

Dr. Haggai spoke with confidence when he talked about his pursuits in life and the goals of his organization: "These people of the Haggai Institute world family don't establish new organizations. They don't start new churches. They don't deploy missionaries. They don't recruit Americans to train nationals in the nonwhite world. They don't produce television or radio programs. They don't sponsor social-service organizations. All of these ideas are fine, but they do not come within the purview of the institute's objective."

He pointed out that when we attach ourselves, like barnacles, to every good program that comes along, we become good for nothing. We become like the man who said he was going to get involved in community life, as his preacher had urged. He joined the Kiwanis Club, the Chamber of Commerce, the Shrine Club, the Garden

Club, the Shuffleboard Club, and the Rolling Stones. He went all out, and in the end he was as ineffective in serving those organizations as he had been in his church work. Why? Because, like the legendary crazy cowboy, he had ridden off in all directions.

Nobody knows the importance of singular focus as well as a laying hen. She produces twenty dozen eggs in a single year. That's all she does, and she does it well. She has become indispensable.

A one-eyed Christian refuses to dilute his effectiveness. He does not dabble in every new fad.

Through prayer and guidance we can be directed toward a single-focus purpose. We will no longer flip-flop like a loose shutter in a windstorm. We will find life exhilarating as we enter into this new phase of our Christian effectiveness. We will no longer quarantine our endeavors or confine our interests to the narrowness of our own mind.

Cyclops Christians, through prayer and with the help of God's power, find definite direction toward doing a super job for the Savior.

Bitter Gall
To Sweet Nectar

"We are now making our approach to Washington National Airport," the voice on the intercom announced. "Please fasten your seat belts and extinguish all cigarettes until we have landed and the aircraft has come to a complete stop."

Did you ever have a nasty day? A day as bitter as a cup of gall?

I was having one. Up at four o'clock. A sixty-mile drive to the airport. A flight I didn't want to make because I absolutely hate to fly. A sick stomach. And now the plane was dropping through heavy clouds to streak down a slick runway in a pouring rain.

But maybe it would get better. My husband was here for a business conference, and I was seeing Washington for the first time. While he worked, I would see the sights. However, instead of a day of pleasure, I found a day of misery and frustration. I stood in a dozen lines waiting to be herded through buildings and past historic spots. I was cold and tired. My feet hurt. I felt that my afternoon had been wasted.

95

That evening we attended a dinner party, hosted by Senator and Mrs. Lawton Chiles, at the Florida House on Capitol Hill. We were met by a photographer taking pictures of all the guests as they arrived. Later, as he had seemingly completed his assignment, he asked me if I was enjoying my visit to Washington.

I told him I was thrilled to be in Washington but unhappy with the way things were going. "I'll never see anything," I complained. "I spent all afternoon standing in lines. I really didn't do much sightseeing because of the crowds."

"We'll have to do something about that," he said. "Would you and your husband like to sit in on the Judiciary hearings tonight? You might see a little excitement." His tone was casual, as though he were inviting us to ride to the corner grocery store.

"Yes, we'd like that," I assured him. Then a wave of embarrassment swept over me, for I was sure I sounded too eager. I hadn't even gone through the motions of asking my husband. I felt like a small girl saying yes to someone offering her an ice-cream cone. I was embarrassed, too, because I didn't even recall this man's name. I had been introduced to him, but names at a dinner party don't always register.

I had assumed that he was a commercial photographer hired to make pictures of the party. Now I realized he must be a man of importance. Because who, this side of a member of Congress, could arrange a seat at those hearings? On television I had seen the long line of people trying to get in.

Everyone at the dinner party seemed to know my new friend on a first-name basis. I picked up his name from listening, "Dev." "He's Dev O'Neill," I was told by the man sitting next to me at dinner. "He's the official photographer for the United States Congress."

Later in the evening, when dinner was over and we rode with him to the Sam Rayburn Building, everyone seemed to know him. The uniformed guard in front of the building directed him to a reserved parking place. As we walked down the crowded halls, important-looking people spoke to him or waved or touched his shoulder in passing. Inside the hearing room, he escorted us to his own reserved seats on the front row.

Dev O'Neill proved to be the perfect host. He was careful to see that we were introduced to the committee chairman and a dozen or so other congressmen. At his elbow we met some of America's top news reporters, commentators, and authors.

Each time Dev O'Neill presented me, he said my name as though I were a celebrity, as though I were the greatest television personality in Florida. That was a night I'll never forget.

How that man had turned my day upside-down! A day that had started with the taste of gall was ending with the flavor of nectar.

When the hearings had recessed and he was driving us back to our hotel, I asked him how he had secured the position of official photographer to Congress. "I created my own job," he said. "There was a need for someone to be directly responsible for covering the events of Congress. I was willing to be on hand, no matter what the time of day or night. It is a tremendously exciting job, but it also carries a heavy load. I guess you could say I got the job through determination and kept it because I was always there."

Does Dev O'Neill like his work? He loves it! His joy is obvious as he poses his subjects and flashes his strobe light. You see perfection every time he moves. He goes about his work with a sense of destiny. And why not? After all, with his camera he is preserving history. Who could ask for a greater opportunity to serve?

Don't all of us start out in life with the determination to reach a certain latitude, longitude, and altitude? Then, somewhere along the way, don't many of us sip from our cup of gall, a cup filled with the bitterness of jealousy, selfishness, envy, and greed? Don't we often forget that we must fill a need, that we must serve in order to reach our greatest altitude?

God does not call two men to serve in exactly the same way. He has made a place for each of us. Dev O'Neill reached his altitude because he answered the call to serve.

Only when we ask God's direction can we find the place that he wants us to work—to serve. That cup of gall can be changed and sweetened only when we dedicate ourselves to total and unselfish service.

Owls' Nests Are for Owls

Everyone who is young at heart likes a good story. One of the most charming in my collection is set in a hotel in New York City. I was awaiting the arrival of Mrs. Lulu Parker Betenson, sister of Butch Cassidy, the notorious outlaw who legend tells us was killed with the Sundance Kid in South America in 1909. Therefore I knew that Lulu was in the twilight years of her life. Later I realized that no one had ever bothered to tell Lulu!

NBC had assigned me to interview Lulu and talk to her about the book she had coauthored on the life of her brother. I was prepared to meet a feeble old lady wearing a basic black dress and flat-heeled shoes. But Lulu was not feeble, her basic black dress turned out to be a chichi original of bright red and yellow print, and she wore shoes with heels higher than mine. She was ninety-one years old.

I shall always remember her opening words: "Young lady, I suppose you think the respectable thing for me to do would be to die. You know, when you are my age

99

you no longer worry about dying. You are afraid that you never will! I have promised my grandchildren and my great-grandchildren that I will 'put them away' in a nice fashion!"

What spunk she generated. The thought occurred to me that most of us, at her age, would find life nothing more than an owl's nest. Just as an owl's nest is made of leftover twigs, string, paper, thread, and sticks, we exist on leftover pieces as we approach the end of our lives. We shrink from death, rather than anticipate it with joy and eagerness as Lulu did.

I wanted to learn more about her brother's life. I had no intention of talking with Lulu about death, but she kept bringing the subject up. From time to time she would refer to her Mormon background, and each time she would mention the matter of dying—almost as if she looked forward to it.

When I was a little girl, I hated to talk about death. I did not want to hear about people dying. The story about Jesus hanging on the cross made me uncomfortable.

Death worries many people. They pick up all sorts of ideas and concepts about it and try to fit them together. And they don't fit. So sincere and earnest Christians often end up with nothing more than a mental owl's nest.

What should you believe?

Jesus said, "Let not your heart be troubled: ye believe in God, believe also in me. In my Father's house are many mansions: if it were not so, I would have told you. I go to prepare a place for you. And if I go and prepare a place for you, I will come again, and receive you unto myself; that where I am, there ye may be also."

Listen to him. Don't let your life become an owl's nest.

Remember, owls' nests are for owls.

Blue Hair and Bald Heads

Did you ever plan your day with a well-organized schedule and have it explode in your face before you even had your morning coffee?

That happened to me one day.

I dashed to the cleaners to pick up my husband's shirts and by the jeweler's for a watch band, then rushed to the post office, intending to go on to the grocery store. With an armload of mail, I returned to my automobile that was parked in the shade of an oak tree, near the entrance to the post office. Quickly I thumbed through the maze of advertisements and bills. Then I ripped open a brown cardboard container marked "book." Here was a book by my friend Dr. Vance Havner, of Greensboro, North Carolina. The title of the book, *Though I Walk through the Valley*, invited further inspection, and I saw it was about the death of his beloved wife, Sarah. I began to read and simply could not lay it down. My day's schedule was ruined.

Two hours later I heard a tap on my window, and my friendly neighborhood policeman suggested that I move my automobile out of the two-hour parking zone. I could not believe I had been sitting there all that time. But it was true. I had read almost the entire book. So I had to skip the rest of my morning errands and get back to my housework.

As I drove down the familiar street leading to my home, I thought about Dr. Havner, the slight, bespectacled gentleman who had blessed so many lives during his sixty years as a minister. His brittle humor and simplicity of style had endeared him to every age group. Not only was he one of my favorite speakers, but his books are among those I treasure most in my library. He has written more than twenty-five of the kind you read over and over, the kind you never tire of.

I first heard him preach in Tampa. Following the meeting, I invited him to appear on my television show. When he arrived for the interview, everyone at the station was eager to meet this dynamic Christian they had heard me talk about. There he stood, a man in his seventies who had recently suffered the loss of his beloved wife and who was still recovering from his heartache. Yet all of us were overwhelmed with his zest for life! The magnetism of his personality touched everyone in the studio.

What a testimony he had lived. And now he was proving that age has nothing to do with years.

Organizations for persons over sixty-five years of age are being started in churches all over the country. They give themselves such names as "The Keenagers," "The Jet Set," and "The Happy Group." These old-timers have been inoculated with "Havnerism." They are young at heart. Each is proof that only when we live close to the Lord are we able to survive life's volcanic eruptions.

Whenever I speak to one of these groups, I see much more than a roomful of blue-haired women and bald-headed men. I see people whose enthusiasm and eagerness are as stimulating as an old-fashioned spring tonic.

That day in the studio, Dr. Havner taught all of us an important lesson. His recovery from a personal loss to good health and high spirits proved the scriptural truth that "surely the very One who created us can heal and restore us." At an age when most men sit retired in front of their television sets, Dr. Havner was keeping a speaking schedule that would have taxed the energies of a man half his age.

When I shook hands with Dr. Havner and thanked him for visiting with me on television, I was reminded of a verse from Proverbs that my father often quoted: "A cheerful heart does good like a medicine, but a broken spirit makes one sick."

No proverb ever hit closer to the mark. Blue hair and bald heads do not curtail our joy and zest for living when we are living in the knowledge that we are doing the Lord's will.

Step Up–Not Down

"We want some help," the young lady told me earnestly. "We need somebody to talk to. You always seem to look at the world through rose-colored glasses, so we thought you could give us some advice."

Two of her friends stood beside her as she spoke to me in the vestibule of our church one Sunday morning. These girls were high school seniors and members of the group my husband and I work with. Their request was not unusual. Young people often come by our house to bare their troubles or tell us some good news or just chat about their latest activities.

We set a date for that afternoon and they arrived on time. Three hours later, as they were leaving the house, the thought crossed my mind, "These kids may not have completely shattered those rose-colored glasses they spoke of, but they certainly made them lose some of their luster."

We had talked about the role of young women in today's world of pot smoking, drug addiction, liberalized views about sex and marriage, and the apparent

obsolescence of our traditional moral standards. Their
conversation had confused me. Their attitudes were a
bit beyond my understanding, and I found difficulty in
grasping their points of view. So I did what I always do
when I have a problem that lies out of reach. I prayed
about it.

The answer to my prayers came by way of an unex-
pected trip to Knoxville and a visit with a long-time
friend, Addie B. Fielden. Although we were not related,
I had called her "Mammo" since I was a little girl.

For more than forty years, she had been teaching
a class of young adult women in her church. And like
my husband and me, she was often called on for advice
and counsel.

She seemed to be in the midst of one such counsel-
ing session when I arrived at her home. She was having
coffee in her living room with an attractive young
woman who appeared to be nervous and ill at ease. I
said my hellos and received a warm hug of welcome. I
quickly excused myself because I could see that I was
interrupting a serious conversation. As I left the room,
I couldn't help overhearing Mammo giving a bit of
strong advice: "You must never stoop to the pleasures
of your husband when it is against the will of the Lord."

That evening after supper, as we were relaxing and
chatting in the gazebo in Mammo's back yard, she told
me about the visitor I had met that afternoon: "She is a
fine young woman. She used to be a pupil of mine, and
now she is teaching her own class of teen-age girls. She
came to tell me that she was resigning all of her church
responsibilities because her conscience is bothering her.
She says she has been forced to go with her husband to
cocktail parties and join with him in other activities that
she does not approve of. Because of his work, she says,

he is living in a style that conflicts with all of her Christian beliefs. She says she must go along with her husband or their marriage will come to an end. Her situation is very sad. She knows that a marriage without God is no marriage at all. No matter which choice she makes, she will be a loser."

After a long silence, Mammo said, "You always pay a high price when you compromise. I think that is the biggest problem facing the young women of America. They are listening to a siren call telling them they should be equal with men—whatever that means. But women are not equal to men. And what is more important, men are not equal to women. Women hold a more exalted position than men. And on those occasions when they do become equal, they are giving up something and are stepping down to man's level.

"I like to teach from Peter Marshall's book, *Mr. Jones, Meet the Master.* He has a chapter which he calls 'Keeper of the Springs,' in which he talks about a woman's role in the world. I have read it to my girls so many times that I can quote it. He says that 'womanhood is a sacred and noble thing, women are of finer clay, are more in touch with the angels of God, and have the noblest function that life affords.'

"I tell the girls that they start life at the top and that when they trifle with their integrity, when they try to 'get with it' by smoking pot and drinking and bed hopping with every boy who comes along, they are lowering themselves. God says we should strive to be lifted up. I guess, in a nutshell, I try to get them to step up and not down."

As I listened to Mammo that evening, I knew what I was going to say to my young friends when I returned home.

Toothbrush or Treasure?

Standing on the knoll between Twin Lakes, Dexter and I could see the billows of black smoke pouring from the rooftop of our friends' home. Lightning had struck while the family was away, and not so much as a toothbrush, tennis ball, or light bulb was salvaged.

What a terrifying experience to return to your home and find everything you own lying in smoldering ashes. Money cannot replace baby pictures, wedding albums, and keepsakes from past days. How heartbreaking and dreadful to see the burial of a family's worldly goods beneath a heap of blackened wood.

Loss of any kind can be a frightening, shocking experience—the farmer's crops devastated by a hailstorm, the voice of a singer destroyed by disease, the child's pet dog killed by a car, the rich lady's diamonds stolen by thieves.

Some people can overcome great loss and walk away from tragedy apparently unscarred and unbruised. Others moan and cry over minor setbacks—

like a neighbor of mine who began to lose his hair.

He became frightened with the thought that he might become bald. He rubbed foul-smelling ointments, perfumed hair oils, and stimulating heat salves into that ever spreading empty spot. Nothing helped. Eventually he lost all of his hair. Because of his misfortune, he has groaned and whined and made himself and everyone around him miserable.

The burning of our friends' home was the worst experience that family had ever known. To the farmer, it was the loss of his crops; to the singer, the loss of his voice; to the boy, the loss of his dog; to the rich lady, the loss of her diamonds. On the other hand, the man who became bald suffered his greatest loss more from humiliation and loss of pride than from the loss of his hair.

Yet the Scriptures tell us that none of these losses is important. If they are not, do any losses really matter?

Yes! Our greatest loss would be our gift of love—our ability to love our fellow man, to love God. Another tragic loss would be our appreciation of all the good in the world around us, or the loss of an open heart that allows joy to enter and flood our soul.

Yes, those would be terrible losses.

Minor losses—great losses. Jesus points out the difference between the two when he says, "Lay not up for yourselves treasures upon earth, where moth and rust doth corrupt, and where thieves break through and steal. But lay up for yourselves treasures in heaven. . . . For where your treasure is, there will your heart be also."

Hand Me That Two-by-Four

"Y'all come! Y'all come!" Bobby Lord sang and strummed his guitar while our feet kept time to the country music beat. Bobby was appearing as a guest on our television show. From the very first song, he urged us to join in the fun. Before long all of us were clapping and stomping and singing with him. He was having so much fun that he did not seem to notice that the tunes sounded more melodic when he sang alone.

Bobby Lord was born in Florida. When he was nineteen he went to Nashville, the country music capital of the world. Immediately captivated by the spirit of the "Nashville sound," he joined the other young people who were trying to make it in the music world. Within ten years he was one of the top performers on the country music circuit.

That morning as we sat in the TV studio, we engaged in the usual informal chitchat. I asked him about his work: "Bobby, there seems to be an explosion of joy sweeping the world for country music. How do you explain the craze for the new sound?"

110

Evidently he had been asked this question before, because he quickly responded, "Everyone is fed up with the plastic world of phonies that we've built. People want something that is really real." He sat quietly for just a moment before he continued: "Country singers don't try to be anything they aren't. They don't try to be glamorous or stuck-up. They just put together a song about how they feel and how they live, and each person who listens feels they are talking about him. We don't try to be subtle. We are country western people. And when we want to pry open a door, we just grab the nearest two-by-four and start prying."

I told Bobby Lord how my interest in country music had developed: "I never knew much about it until one day my husband hired a country and western band to play during an all-day celebration where he was introducing the new automobile models for the year. The big names in that field of show business were not then included among my household words. I wasn't a fan."

I explained how my attitude had changed when I dropped by the showroom to see how the day was going. It was certainly going well. I had never seen such a huge crowd in our small town. I later learned that more than ten thousand people had visited the new-car showing. I wondered what had inspired so many people to turn out on such a hot, sweltering day.

"Then I heard the music," I said. "It sounded real, just like you said, Bobby. And the members of the band seemed to bubble over as they sang and played. And I met the performers, Carl Smith, Johnny Carver, Arlene Harden, Jack Reno, and Johnny Russell. I stayed that afternoon until they had played the last number—three hours overtime. I marveled at this group. They loved their work. They were young and outgoing. They had not shown one moment of irritation or made a single complaining remark. They smiled and spread happiness and joy in spite of the 115-degree heat on the parking lot, in spite of the extra hours, and in spite of the mob of sticky-fingered children and slow-moving old people who crowded around for autographs."

Bobby listened politely while I related my experience. Then suddenly our conversation turned to another topic.

"There's another thing," Bobby said. "We aren't afraid to talk about Jesus. Everybody knows who we mean when we mention Jesus, so we don't talk about God or the Holy Spirit. We make it simple and talk about Jesus. The people understand. How do we know they understand? Because they tell us so."

I understood what Bobby was saying. He was right. Our society has become so sophisticated that we have complicated everything from filling in our income-tax forms, to assembling a child's modern toy, to telling others about Jesus Christ.

At that point, the TV director called Bobby to the studio. Bobby hesitated long enough to say, "We are proud of the way we are. Proud of our raising. We are proud that we believe in God, hard work, and the basic decency of human beings."

He left me with a head full of thoughts to sort out. I had enjoyed my glimpse into the world of the country singer. It was not a world of chocolate cake with pink foam frosting. It was not a goody-goody world. I had seen a real world, a world filled with the same problems as my world, but also a world brimming with love and caring.

Along with his friends, Bobby Lord was simply

grabbing that old two-by-four, prying those doors open, and inviting Jesus to come into his world.

As I drove home that night, I could still hear Bobby in my mind, prying open the door for all of us, as he sang, "Y'all come! Y'all come!"

The Cat's Meow

"Aarrk! Aarrk! Aarrk!" I heard the familiar croaking sound of the Great Blue Heron as it approached our fishing dock. I grabbed the bag of stale bread and raced for the lakefront. But I was too late.

"Little Kat" had been waiting under the seagrape plant and had already managed to scare away the heron. It now circled high above a stand of bamboo waiting for my appearance before attempting another landing. Little Kat continued to meow so loudly that a fisherman two docks away was laughing at the confused scene. But the heron has learned that once I am on the dock, it is safe, and it swoops down for its handout, completely ignoring the cat. I go through this ritual with bird and cat nearly every day.

Little Kat is an odd-eyed calico with a searing jealousy for the heron. With her one golden topaz eye and one as blue as sapphire, she stands vigil each noon waiting for the heron to fly down for its lunch from its nesting place in the top of a hundred-year-old cypress. The moment Kat spies her enemy, she meows in protest, because she sees it as a threat to her pampered life-style. She has reigned as the only pet in our household for eleven years, and she is not about to share her domain with a hungry heron.

Kat must really hate that huge bird, because she is irritable for hours after it comes to the dock to feed on the breadcrusts I throw to it. On those days that the heron finds enough fish to curb its appetite, it skips the free lunch, and Little Kat purrs with contentment. In her cunning feline mind she thinks she has rid herself of her long-legged enemy. But whenever it shows up, she becomes irritable again.

Foolish, isn't it? But is the cat-heron episode any more foolish than many of the person-person situations we see every day?

I recently eavesdropped on a conversation between a young secretary, Patricia McMillan, and her next-door neighbor. The neighbor was telling Patricia how a fellow worker had become a "thorn in my flesh." "I cannot stand to work with that man any longer," she insisted. "He deliberately sets traps to make me look inefficient. I loved my job until he came to work in the office, but now I would give it all up for some peace."

In a manner far more mature than her years, Patricia replied, "There would only be someone else at your next job just like him. I know it's hard to ignore him, when he continually upsets you. But why not try a magic formula that I use? It was discovered more than two thousand years ago and pertains to people who insist on 'bugging' you. Excuse me a minute and I'll get it and read it to you."

She was gone in the house for only a few minutes. When she returned, she had a copy of *The Living Bible* in her hands. She turned to Luke 6:22 and read slowly,

"What happiness it is when others hate you and exclude you and insult you and smear your name. . . . When that happens, rejoice! Yes, leap for joy! . . . you will be in good company—the ancient prophets were treated that way too!"

That is a paraphrase of one of the Beatitudes of Jesus that we have known since we were little.

Several months after that conversation, Patricia's neighbor told her she had received a promotion with a sizable raise. "I would have been foolish to leave that job," she said. "I love it. I really found happiness in my work that day when you talked to me. That man I told you about became terribly annoyed when he could no longer 'bug' me, and he went off to pester someone else."

Yes, Patricia's neighbor learned the benefits of ignoring the insolence of her office colleague. Just as my friend the heron knows it will be fed if it ignores the cat when I stand on the dock.

And what about you when you hear the "cat's meow" in the bushes? Ignore it. Learn to ignore the criticisms, jealousies, and petty annoyances that come your way, and as Jesus said, ". . . leap for joy! . . . you will be in good company—the ancient prophets were treated that way too!"

The Eye

What fun! What excitement! The Reynolds' air-boat skimmed over the lake at sixty miles an hour. The eerie beauty of the moss-draped cypress along the shore was enhanced by the faint twinkling of a few scattered stars. The roar of the powerful motor drowned out the occasional flip of a fish's tail and the songs of the frogs that made their homes among the lily pads. Then the engine was silent. We were drifting, and our ears gradually adjusted to the peace and quiet of the summer night.

"Here's what we're looking for," our guide said. He whispered so that we would not disturb the frogs that we had come to gig along the edge of the lake. Now that we were close to shore, the blackness wrapped itself around us.

Then suddenly the powerful spotlight flashed on. A display of shining jewels lay before us like rose and ruby zircons lying in a Tiffany tray. All around us the tiny specks gleamed and sparkled.

"Those are the eyes of the frogs," he explained.

117

"You can tell their maturity by the distance between their eyes. The closer together, the younger the frog."

Then he showed me how to get the frogs. "While you're gigging," he instructed me, "I'll pole the boat slowly through the lily pads. Hit the frog with a quick jab. That's all there is to it. You'll catch on after you've missed a couple. Then, when you get one, take him off the gig and put him in the gunny sack. Let's go."

During the next two hours we speared more than sixty-five frogs—the makings of a gourmet dinner for a dozen hungry guests.

Later, as we said good-night to our guide, I remarked, "I didn't know a frog's eyes were shiny."

"Oh, they're not," he explained. "What you saw was the reflection of our own spotlight. You weren't looking into the eyes of the frogs. I've often wondered about that. I think if I ever looked a frog directly in the eye, I would be too tenderhearted to gig him." He laughed a little as we waved our good-byes.

As we drove home, I recalled an experience my husband often speaks of—about looking in people's eyes. Several years ago he was flying home from a business trip. As he settled down in the huge jetliner and strapped himself into his seat, he found himself sitting next to a young man in uniform. It was obvious from the display of ribbons on the soldier's jacket that he had been on duty in a war zone.

"It looks as though you've seen quite a bit of action," my husband remarked. "Arc you on your way home?"

"Yes," the soldier replied. "I've spent three years in Vietnam, but I'm on terminal leave now and I'm on my way to visit my parents."

As they continued to chat, my husband drew out

bits and pieces of the young man's story. He had served
as a medical corpsman attached to a field hospital. It
had been his job to go into the field to give first aid to
the injured and help bring them into the hospital.

"I'll bet you're glad to be leaving it all behind you,"
my husband said.

"I wish I were," the soldier confided, "but it isn't
that easy. I am leaving Vietnam behind me, that's true
enough. But I'm afraid some of the misery will stay with
me as long as I live. As a medic, my job was to help the
men who had a chance to live. If we found a man who
was dying, we tried to ease his pain, pass him by, and go
on to a man who had a chance to live. Sometimes that
was a hard decision to make. In order to be able to make
that choice, we were taught an ironclad rule. We were
told never to look into the eyes of a man who was dying.
If we ever did, we were told, we wouldn't be able to
leave him on the battlefield. Well, I did it. I did it twice."
Then, with tears streaming down his face, he implored,
"Mister, don't ever look into the eyes of a man who is
dying. His agony will haunt you as long as you live."

This agony can pass from generation to generation.

Thus the agony of Jesus haunts the souls of men
today. As he hung dying on the cross, his eyes searched
those of all who passed, and they looked at his. Those
who came to scoff or jeer or gloat stood transformed.
Those who came in reverence and sadness and shame
were lifted to a higher plane. His dying eyes cried out,
"Remember me and tell the world. Go ye, therefore,
and teach all nations. . . ."

Go, Gator!

Nearly every day about noon, an alligator crawls up on my lakefront beach for a bit of sunbathing. It is not large, as alligators go—about four feet long. I have not tried to make friends with it. I have not given it a nickname. I do not go down on the beach and sunbathe with it. I don't feed it.

One day when I was watching from my window, I saw my neighbor's son playing on the beach with his little dog. They both were somewhat wary of the alligator. The boy stayed away from it, but the dog approached within sniffing distance. The little alligator appeared to be asleep. It never moved. Then, trying to get a little action I suppose, the boy threw a rotten orange at it. He scored a direct hit, and the alligator showed its anger by snapping at the dog. For a few moments I was frightened. I know it scared the boy, because he never bothered that alligator again.

I want my attitude toward alligators understood. I am not anti-alligator. They have their place in Florida swamps and lakes and rivers. On the other hand, I am not going to pet them or invite them into my home.

I have my own way of dealing with my alligator. To begin with, I know it's there. I recognize that fact. I don't ignore it. If I did, I might step on it sometime and get into serious trouble. I don't pet it, either, because I have always heard that you can't tame an alligator. As long as it doesn't bother me, I don't bother it. If it wants to sun itself on my little beach when I'm not around, that's its business. But when I want to use the beach, that's my business. And since I have the upper hand in the matter, I take it. I have an old rake handle about five feet long that I keep on the beach. All I have to do is poke the gator a couple of times with my big stick and it hits the water and swims away. I am sure it is more afraid of me than I am of it.

All of which is my way of telling about the late Dr. James P. Rodgers and his address at my high school graduation. He titled his speech "Alligators," and he described the fears in our lives as "modern-day alligators." That was a long time ago, but every time I see that alligator sunning itself on my beach, I remember Dr. Rodgers and what he said.

Of course, I can't quote him exactly, but I do remember how he talked about fears. He said people have all sorts of fears. He told us about people who suffer from claustrophobia, the fear of confined spaces, and hydrophobia, the fear of water. He mentioned a man who was a victim of hypnophobia—he was afraid to go to sleep at night. He explained that the list was almost endless: acrophobia, the fear of high places; misophobia, the fear of dirt and germs; and a rare one, erythrophobia, the fear of blushing.

Then he touched his central theme and explained that fears are like alligators. They are ugly. They don't contribute anything of value. They sometimes fool you by lying around as though they are asleep, but pounce on you when you step too close. He said that when you discover you have a certain fear, admit it. Recognize that it is there. Then leave it alone. Don't bother it if it doesn't bother you. But when it gets in the way of your own desires or progress, take a stick and drive it away.

As I said, that's the way I treat my alligator, and that's the way I treat my fears.

I don't have many fears now. When I was little, I was afraid of the dark. And strangely enough, I was afraid of railroad locomotives. They frightened me and caused me to cringe as they roared past with steam hissing out of their sides and their whistles blowing.

Today, the only fear I can think of is my fear of flying. I have made up my mind to conquer it. Flying once terrified me. Now I just hate it. I dislike every minute I am off the ground, but since I do fly now and then, I have learned to drive my fear out of my mind. I can't drive it out with a stick, like I drive my alligator off my beach, but I use something just as handy.

Each time I board a plane, I remember what David said when he was afraid: "I cried unto the Lord and he delivered me from all my fears."

In spite of my fears, I have always landed safely.

I'm in Love

Good morning!

I am sitting under a magnolia tree near the corner of my house. The sun is beginning to come up over the lake to replace the shadows of night with golden patches of shimmering topaz.

I often begin my day here when I want absolute quiet to think and write. What I am about to say will be a personal message—about myself.

I did not sleep well last night, because I kept hearing in my mind the voice of a friend telling me her troubles. Her marriage is ending in divorce. She visited us last night until long after midnight. As she was leaving, she turned to me and said, "You have a twenty-year marriage, the same as we. Why is yours so different?"

We have been asked that question often during the past several months as we have seen the tragedy of divorce take its toll from among our close circle of friends. These friends are Christians who have centered their homes around the church. At least one counselor had placed the blame on the "twenty-year syndrome."

The heartbreak, scars, and hurt that my friend's divorce was bringing to us had made me reflect on my own marriage.

This morning I asked myself, "Why *is* our marriage different?"

One clue may be found in an accident that happened early in our marriage. It left such an impact that it still influences our relationship.

Dexter and I had been childhood sweethearts, but we dated other classmates during high school and college, then waited until we were twenty-six before we married. During that first year, we moved into a beautiful new home. Life was perfect. Dexter had brought to me everything a bride could wish for—a marvelous sense of humor, enthusiasm for our future, a steadfast faith in God. He seemed to appreciate all of the everyday happenings around us. He showed a devoted interest in me as an individual. He made me feel important. We were experiencing unbounded happiness.

Then, shortly before we were to celebrate our first anniversary, I became critically ill. My problem was diagnosed as fibromyositis, an inflammation around the heart. After several weeks in the local hospital, with no improvement, I was moved to the Shands Teaching Hospital at the University of Florida in Gainesville—more than a hundred miles away.

Suddenly my whole being crumbled and fell apart. Fear dominated every thought. Would I die? Would I become an invalid for Dexter to care for from now on? Why was I being moved to another hospital? Would I ever see Dexter again?

But of course! Of course he came. He drove up to see me every night after he finished work. One evening after I had been there about a week, he found me crying incoherently when he arrived.

He tried to calm me, but I was sobbing uncontrollably. He picked up the Bible that was lying on my bedside table and said he was going to read to me.

Even though we had always read the Bible and prayed together at the end of each day, I screamed at him, "Don't read to me tonight! I can't stand it. I don't want to hear it!"

He quietly ignored my protests and turned to Psalms. "We missed the whole key last night," he said, "when we were reading the Twenty-third Psalm together. We were supposed to go back a little and read the opening of the Twenty-second Psalm first."

I'll always remember that moment. I can hear his voice even now as he read to me, "My God! My God, why have you forsaken me?"

"That's me. That's me," I moaned as tears overflowed my red and swollen eyes.

He continued to read softly, and I heard his words: "Oh, my God, I cry in the daytime, but thou hearest not."

Now I was almost hysterical. I grabbed Dexter by the arm and pushed my face into his hands. Tears dripped from my face to the pages of the Holy Book he was holding. "That's me. That's me," I sobbed. "He was writing about me."

Dexter's voice was choking as he said, "Yes, honey, that was written for you. David knew the same depth of sorrow that you are experiencing. And he wrote something else for you too. I am going to read it to you now as though he were talking to you in person. Listen."

"The Lord is your shepherd," Dexter read, "and you have everything you need." He was right. Immediately the message belonged to me. Only to me.

He read on. His voice was stronger now. "He maketh you to lie down in green pastures. He leadeth you beside the still waters." I felt a soothing calmness embrace me. "He restoreth your soul." I could sense the confidence that was coming into his voice. My fear began to drain away. I was viewing my illness from a new perspective.

His words fairly boomed at me as he read, "You will fear no evil." Then in his own words he added, "Now, honey, you see. You are told not to be afraid. That is your only trouble. Not your real sickness, but fear. Please be quiet and listen so that you can hear what he is telling you."

He repeated, "You will fear no evil."

As though a voice were coming from a distance, I heard my own words, "I will fear no evil. I will fear no evil."

I slept that night. I rested for the first time since I had been moved to Gainesville. I slept all night without moving and without the aid of a sleeping pill. When I woke up, Dexter was still sitting there. For the first time in my life, I knew the true meaning of love and devotion and sacrifice. The thought swept over me that truly this man was a part of me now, and nothing could ever pull us apart. I whispered with more meaning than I had ever put into the words, "I love you."

Dexter smiled and said, "Me too."

Then I told him about going to sleep. "The last thing I remember about last night," I said, "was hearing you say, 'Though I walk through the valley of the shadow of death.'"

"That's right," he said. "Remember that. It is *through* the valley, not *in* the valley or *beside* the valley. The psalm says *through* the valley. He means that no matter how dark the season, you will go through the valley. You are God's child, and whatever comes, you will be able to bear up under it. He will lead you beside the still, calm waters, and you can see the sunshine coming to meet you."

From that moment on, my recovery came rapidly. With the return of my health came a trust in God that has never wavered.

And my love for Dexter? How can you measure your feelings for someone who took you by the hand and comforted you and led you through the valley?

The sun is higher now. I must pick up my pencil and writing pad and leave the shelter of my magnolia tree. Dexter will be getting up soon, and I want to have his breakfast ready for him.

But what about that question: Why is our marriage different?

I don't know exactly. I am sure it is no different from millions of others. Yet it must be different from my friend's, because hers has fallen apart.

Maybe ours is different because we both remember that day a long time ago when we walked together through the valley.

Yes, Dexter and I have walked "through the valley" many times since then. But we always have stood side by side holding hands with the knowledge that the Lord is our Shepherd. Never have we been afraid again.

Thanks

To Winston K. Pendleton, my literary guardian angel, who spent endless hours separating the wheat from the chaff in my vignettes of joy.

To Dr. and Mrs. Milburn Calhoun, my friends and publisher, whose belief in me sparked this project and whose encouragement throughout has been constant.

To Catherine Marshall LeSourd, who encouraged me joyously in my writing with these words: "Let me wish you God's real help with this major undertaking and his blessings on it all the way from beginning to end."